A–Z OF FRENCH RAILWAYS

PLACES - PEOPLE - HISTORY

Patrick Bennett

AMBERLEY

First published 2019

Amberley Publishing
The Hill, Stroud, Gloucestershire, GL5 4EP
www.amberley-books.com

ISBN 978 1 4456 9097 1 (print)
ISBN 978 1 4456 9098 8 (ebook)

British Library Cataloguing in Publication Data.
A catalogue record for this book is available from the British Library.

Origination by Amberley Publishing.
Printed in Great Britain.

Contents

Introduction

The railways of France are unlike any other, both in terms of their extraordinary variety and the excellence of their engineering. In many ways French railways pursued a path quite different to their neighbours. In the first place, French steam locomotives tended to be much more sophisticated in their engineering; the French were early adopters of compounding, for example, little used in either Germany or Britain. Widespread electrification and dieselisation made early appearances in France and in the modern era we have the TGV network, unequalled anywhere in the world.

Another major difference is the way that the railways developed, with far more state control over which railways were built and where they were built. In the latter part of the nineteenth century the French government was very much aware of the importance of the railways in times of war, and much development was governed by this concern; indeed, the railways played a central role during the two world wars.

Perhaps the greatest difference between the French railways and systems elsewhere was in the construction in the late nineteenth and early twentieth centuries of the system of *départemental* railways, amounting to some 20,000 kilometres of mostly metre-gauge lines. These railways were built over an extraordinarily short period and disappeared during an equally brief period, leaving almost nothing of this once vast system today. Thus, the railways of France present a fascinatingly varied history, and in this book I have tempted to give a flavour of that remarkable story.

The author would like to thank the following person for permission to use copyright material in this book: Graham Skinner for the photographs taken at Paris, Dijon, Andelot and Coubert. The photographs by Ben Brooksbank taken at Le Mans, Chaumont, Limoges, Sommesous, Abbeville and Chalons-sur-Marne are reproduced under the Creative Commons Share-alike licence. Every attempt has been made to seek permission for copyright material used in this book; however, if I have inadvertently used copyright material without permission/acknowledgement I apologise and will make the necessary correction at the first opportunity.

A

Accidents

The Etat line heading south from Angers crossed the various arms of the Loire on three metal bridges (Les Ponts-de-Cé). On 4 August 1907 train No. 407, the Angers–Poitiers omnibus, derailed as it started to cross the first of these bridges. The locomotive (2-4-0 No. 2517 *Moissac*) together with a *fourgon* and one carriage plunged through the deck of the bridge into the river. Twenty-five people died. The line was not reopened until July 1908.

1. Catastrophe de Chemin de fer de Montreuil-Bellay
(23 Novembre 1911)
Un train de voyageurs précipité dans la rivière « Le Thouet »
Les onze rescapés sur le seul wagon qui n'a pas eté submergé
Photo H Collet, édit.
Reprod. interdite

Four years later there was to be another accident involving an Angers–Poitiers train crossing a river bridge. The line from Angers crossed the River Thouet on a bridge just to the south of the town of Montreuil-Bellay before curving up northwards to join the line from Saumur at the station. On 23 November, while the train omnibus No. 405 was crossing the bridge, the central pier, undermined by floodwater, collapsed plunging the two locomotives, two *fourgons* and three carriages into the river. Two of the carriages were swept away, with one being found 800 metres downstream. Fourteen people died. A group of eleven survivors, sitting on the side of their upturned carriage, had to wait 9 hours before being rescued. The bridge reopened the following year. On the 100th anniversary of the accident, the commune of Vaudelnay, the location of the last station the train passed through before the accident, erected a commemorative plaque on one of the bridge abutments.

St-Valery was the scene of two very similar accidents. The first, which occurred on 31 March 1902, concerned passenger train No. 801. Being unable to stop, the train ploughed through a *fourgon*, which it reduced to matchwood, then through the buffers and into the waiting room. There were no fatalities. The engine concerned was Ouest 0-4-2 No. 422, one of the series 401–423 built by Buddicom between 1847 and 1850. Reboilered between 1885 and 1890, the last of the class was withdrawn in 1922.

A far more serious accident occurred on 17 January 1945 when a train carrying American troops was unable to stop and passed clean through the station building. Fifty GIs were killed and 200 injured. The locomotive appears to be a 'dub-dee' (WD).

On 20 April 1913 the 'catastrophe d'Ancenis' occurred. A landslip blocking the line caused the *rapide* Paris–Nantes to derail and plunge into the Loire.

One of the most famous of railway photographs is this one of Ouest 2-4-0 locomotive No. 721, which has come to grief at Montparnasse station. The engine was hauling a Granville–Paris express when it failed to stop upon arrival at the station. It passed through the buffers and over the concourse, before crashing through the end wall and landing in the street below. A woman selling newspapers in the street below was killed. The engine was returned to the workshops where it was found to be little damaged.

Tramways de l'Ardèche

In his book *Les Tramways à Vapeur et Electriques de l'Ardèche*, Henri Domengie begins with the following words (translation): 'Operated by four different administrations from 1910 to 1929, the network of the TA knew an existence brief and eventful. Badly conceived, badly equipped, badly run, badly administered, serving a region sparsely populated, it very rapidly went bankrupt.' Even among a railway sector notorious for the financial problems of its companies and the brevity of the existence of its networks, the TA was something of a special case.

Even after the building of the Privas and Le Teil–Alès lines, the Bas-Vivarais was still badly served by railway lines. It was against this background that the *département* decided on a metre-gauge network of lines of *intérêt local*. The meeting of the *conseil général* on 15 September 1901 decided on the following eight lines: Le Pouzin to Privas, Privas to Aubenas, Aubenas to Uzer, Uzer to Les Vans, Les Vans to St-Paul-le-Jeune, a branch from La Croizette d'Uzer to Largentière, Ruoms to Vallon and Peray to Vernoux.

Twelve 2-6-0 tanks were bought from Piguet at Lyon. Nos 4, 5 and 6 were allocated to the St-Peray line, No. 9 to Vallon, and the remaining eight to Le Pouzin–St-Paul. Much later, two CFD Pinguely locomotives were loaned to the TA for operation of the St-Peray line. In 1912 two two-axled *automotrices* were purchased from Exshaw & Co., the successors to Purrey (see page 62), for use on the Croizette d'Uzer–Largentière and Ruom–Vallon lines. By 1914 they were out of use. In the 1920s a Saurer *autorail* was purchased – type ADVF. Problems with derailments led to the leading axle being replaced by a bogie. The railway started life with a total of nineteen carriages of various seating combinations, eight *fourgon-postes*, and the usual array of freight wagons.

From the start things did not go well for the TA. Not all the work of building and equipping the stations had been completed before the opening. As an example, none of the stations had name boards. The locomotives purchased were not up to the job and were insufficient in number. As a result, utilisation was intensive and there were frequent breakdowns, for which no replacement locomotives were available. Trains were simply cancelled. By 1911 the company started to hire some of the Orenstein and Koppel engines used in construction of the line. Despite this, the situation continued to worsen. On 2 February 1914 passenger services were withdrawn between Le Pouzin and Aubenas, on 24 February they stopped between Ruoms and Vallon, and on 8 March all passenger services ceased, apart from those on the St-Peray–Vernoux line. In June, a strike by staff at the *depôt* at Bellevue (they had not been paid) led to the withdrawal of freight services as well, except on the St-Peray line.

In the early part of the First World War a few troop transports were run and the St-Peray line continued with a single daily return service. In October 1915 forty freight wagons were transferred to the Voies Ferrées du Dauphiné, where they were to be used for the transport of war material. In 1917, with the exception of the St-Peray line and a few metres here and there, the entire track of the TA was requisitioned by the army. Several carriages, turntables and other items were also taken.

At the conclusion of the war the *département* was anxious to reinstate the railway, but accepted that the sections Le Pouzin–Aubenas, Ruoms–Vallon, and La Croizette–Largentière were no longer viable. Track was relayed between Aubenas and St-Paul, but it proved impossible for the *conseil général* to reach an agreement with the original concessionaires of the railway, and in 1923 they were replaced by the Chemins de Fer Départementaux (CFD). Despite their best efforts the deficits continued to accumulate, and in 1926 the Aubenas–Uzer section went over to road transport, followed, in 1928, by the St-Peray–Vernoux line. In 1929 the remaining section between Uzer and St-Paul-le-Jeune went over to a mixed road/rail system, while trains were briefly reinstated on the St-Peray line. At the end of that year all rail traffic ceased. Henceforth, passengers would be conveyed by the buses of the Sociéte Générale des Transports Départementaux. The tramway was no more.

In 1910 the inaugural Tramways de l'Ardèche train emerges from the tunnel under the Col d'Escrinet.

B

A Brief Life

The pressure for a line from Carmaux to Vindrac came from the inhabitants of both Cordes and of Carmaux, who were anxious for a more rapid route to Bordeaux and the capital. The concession was awarded to the Midi in 1883; however, nothing happened until 1905 when, as a result of further pressure from local representatives, the line was declared of *utilité publique*. By 1908 plans were approved for a line of 26 km, following the valley of the Cérou, with stations at Monestiés, La Salle, Campes and Cordes. Nothing further happened until 1915 when, with the help of a thousand German prisoners of war, construction work finally started. By 1923 the infrastructure was mostly completed. The *ouvrages d'art* included thirteen bridges across the Cérou and a tunnel of 138 metres situated between Monestiés and Carmaux.

A complication arose in 1924 when it was decided that trains from Carmaux should have Lexos as their destination, rather than Vindrac, thus avoiding the need for passengers to change at both Vindrac and Lexos when making onward journeys. In order to facilitate this arrangement, it was deemed necessary to increase the goods and servicing facilities at Lexos, this work taking place until 1927. Between 1929 and 1931 the track was laid and the four stations were built.

By this time the prospect of any substantial business arising from the line had long receded and the Midi was reluctant to start services. They proposed that the line be used for freight only. Eventually it was decided to operate the service using *autorails,* but nothing happened until 31 May 1937 when the first train ran. Initially the service of three return trains per day was provided using Renault VH and Michelin *autorails*. The 'Michelines' were found to have a tendency to derail at speed and were replaced by Renaults. The journey time from Carmaux to Vindrac was 47 minutes. Notice that the trains ran only to Vindrac and not, as originally planned, to Lexos, thus rendering the works carried out at the latter station, and the consequent delay, completely pointless. Tickets were sold on the train since none of the stations were staffed, and there was no possibility for trains to cross, being a single line without any crossing loops.

In 1938 the service was reduced to two daily returns. Connections at Vindrac were not good, with passengers having to wait up to 4 hours for a connection to Paris. The end could not be long delayed and the SNCF, which had succeeded the PO-Midi, which had in turn succeeded the Midi, ended the passenger service on 1 July 1939. This line, which had first been mentioned in the plan Freycinet in 1879 and had thus been in gestation for fifty-eight years, was open for exactly twenty-five months, a record for French railways. A few freight trains ran after the closure to passengers, but the track, needed elsewhere, was lifted in 1945, save for a 2.5-km section at the Carmaux end, which was used for trains to a chemical company. This closed in 1970.

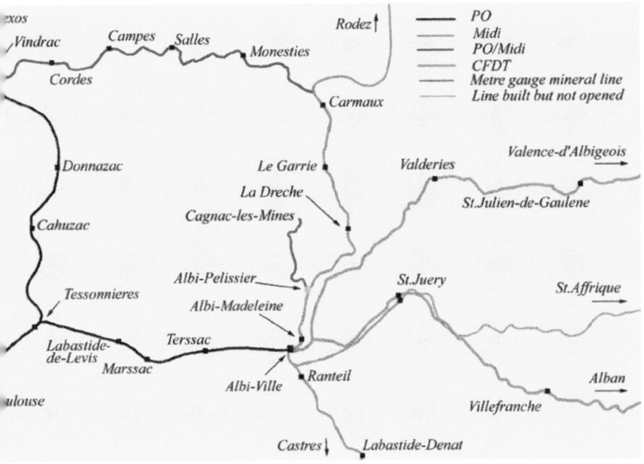

Above left: The Carmaux–Vindrac line is shown in blue.

Above right: The station of Monestiés on the ephemeral Carmaux–Vindrac line.

Bugatti

Bugatti is a name more usually associated with expensive racing cars; however, in 1933 Ettore Bugatti produced his first *autorail* for the Etat network in France. This was an unusual machine by any standard. The body, which could seat forty-eight, sat on two four-axle bogies. The wheel centres and rims were of steel, between which was a cushion of rubber. Power was provided by four eight-cylinder, in-line, 12.7-litre Bugatti Royale petrol engines, which were each rated at 200 hp at 2,000 rpm for railway use. The engines were placed transversely in the centre of the unit and drove the middle pair of axles in each bogie by a system of shafts.

In all, Bugatti produced eighty-eight *autorails* in six different versions. These were supplied to the Etat, PLM, Alsace-Lorraine system and to SNCF. During the Second World War, due to the scarcity of fuel, the Bugattis were taken out of service. Running began again after the cessation of hostilities, but by the end of the 1950s the trains were seen as old technology. The last Bugatti ran in 1958. One of the Etat's examples is preserved at the Cité du Train at Mulhouse.

The publicity poster shows one of the PLM's Bugatti *Couplages*, which consisted of a power car and trailer.

C

Chapelon

André Chapelon is probably the foremost contender to be nominated as the greatest steam locomotive engineer of the twentieth century. His achievements were extraordinary, and the only sadness is that he was at the height of his powers when the decision was made, at least in France, that the future did not reside with steam locomotion.

After a short spell with the PLM and a period outside the railway industry, Chapelon joined the PO in 1925. His ideas on improving efficiency and power output were put into practice with the rebuilding of one of the PO 3500 class of Pacifics. The engine chosen was No. 3566 – such a poor locomotive that it was nicknamed 'Cholera' by the enginemen. The engine emerged from the works in 1929 and it was clear that a remarkable transformation had been achieved. In March 1931, No. 3566 took over a Paris–Bordeaux special at Les Aubrais and completed the 462-km journey in 4 hours and 26 minutes, giving an average speed in excess of 100 kph. Another trial took place the following March when No. 3566, now renumbered 3701, hauled a Paris–Redon train of 435 tonnes, once again taking over at Les Aubrais, and achieved the remarkable average speed for the journey in excess of 120 kph. Line speeds had been temporarily raised for the occasion. Power output had been raised from 1,800 hp to 3,000 hp, while at the same time giving an economy of 25 per cent. In the light of these findings the rest of the class was rebuilt. So sensational were these results that they were to have a major effect on locomotive design – not just in France, but beyond as well.

Chapelon's next major achievement was the rebuilding of a PO 4500 Pacific as a 4-8-0. This rebuilding was no less successful than that of the Class 3500. On trial, the first rebuilt engine, No. 4521, was delivering 4,000 hp at 70 mph. Chapelon had many more successes, among which was the rebuilding of the Etat's 4-8-2, No. 241.101, a very poor performer. Chapelon rebuilt it as a 4-8-4 and the results of this rebuilding were astonishing. Now numbered 242A 1, this engine could easily handle trains of 700 or 800 tonnes on heavily graded routes with 4,000 hp at the drawbar.

As engineer-in-chief of the nationalised SNCF, Chapelon put forward a plan for a fleet of modern, efficient steam locomotives. However, the decision had been made that electrification was the way forward and these plans were never to see the light of day.

No. 3566 in its rebuilt form.

Chapelon stands in front of the unique No. 242A 1.

Tacot des Crouillottes*

At the beginning of the twentieth century Schneider at le Creusot needed to find a means of disposing of the waste from its furnaces, which amounted to some 20,000 tonnes per month. The solution adopted was to dump the waste on a nearby hill. To this end a standard-gauge line was built in 1905 ascending the hill to the dumping ground. Motive power was in the hands of Schneider's 0-6-0 tanks, an engine running at each end of the trains. Unloading was initially carried out by hand, but later steam cranes were employed. During the First World War, the summit of the hill was used for testing some of the artillery pieces produced by Schneider. The guns were moved by train, with, in the case of the 320-mm canon, four locomotives being required. The line ceased operation in the 1950s, after which the rails were lifted.

At the end of the 1980s a group of local enthusiasts rebuilt the line to a 60-cm gauge, and by 1990 5.2 km of track was in place, making a circular route round the hill. In 1998 the line was extended to a newly built terminus adjacent to Le Creusot-Ville station, giving a total length of 10 km. The railway runs in concert with the Parc des Combes, an amusement park situated on top of the hill, and where the other main station is located. Trains run through most of the year, with steam in July and August. Motive power is in the hands of two Deutsche Feldbahn 0-8-0 tanks as well as a collection of shunters. The railway claims uniqueness in that no other private 60-cm railway involves a climb of 110 metres from terminus to summit. It may have another claim to fame in being the only 60-cm railway to run a dining train.

Feldbahn 0-8-0 No. 1239 hauls a train up the hill in July 2012.

*In the past the hill was the focus of an annual pilgrimage, with the pilgrims wearing a small cross on their chests. In local patois these crosses were known as *crouillottes*, which by association came to be the name of the hill and subsequently of the railway.

D

The Life and Mysterious Death of Rudolf Diesel

Rudolf Diesel was born in Paris in 1858 of German parents. In 1870 the outbreak of the Franco-Prussian war caused the Diesel family to decamp to London. In November of that year the Diesels moved to Augsburg in Bavaria. Here and in Munich, Diesel received a technical education and started to focus his attention on the major inadequacy of the steam engine – the fact that so little of the potential energy in the fuel was converted to usable energy. He was intrigued by Joseph Mollet's *briquet*, which the latter described in his 1804 paper *'L'inflammation des matières combustibles, et l'Apparition d'une vive lumière, obtenues par la seule compression de l'air'*. In other words, air compressed to a sufficiently high pressure would ignite some materials.

In 1879, Diesel obtained a placement to continue his studies with Sulzer at Winterthur. After this, he moved to Paris where he took up a position as a concessionaire for refrigeration equipment. In the meantime, he continued to develop his ideas on what we now know as the compression-ignition engine. In 1893, with his plans finalised, he took out his first patent. In a collaboration with Krupp at Augsburg Diesel manufactured his first single-cylinder machine. On 10 August it was tried out for the first time and exploded. Undaunted by this near fatal experience, Diesel continued to develop his machine, which, in 1897, he was ready to demonstrate in front of representatives from Deutz, Krupp, Sulzer and other notables from the field of engineering. This single-cylinder four-stroke engine driving a flywheel was 26.8 per cent thermically efficient – a considerable improvement on the thermal efficiency of the steam engine. This engine is now on permanent display in the Deutsches Museum, Munich. Diesel sold licences to build, as well as the machines themselves, which were built at Augsburg. He entered an agreement with Sulzer to give them exclusive use of his patents in Switzerland. Diesel became a very rich man and lived in some luxury in Munich.

(Although we are now accustomed to diesel engines using petroleum derivatives as fuel, in fact Diesel tried out a number of other substances. These included coal powder, palm, peanut and fish oils, and almost unbelievably, whey!)

Early use of his engines was mainly to be found in marine applications, but in 1906 the company Diesel-Kloze-Sulzer was formed to explore the possibility of the employment of Diesel engines for railway use. In 1912 the first locomotive was produced. This 2B2 was equipped with a 1,000-hp V4 two-stroke engine mounted transversely and driving the motor axles directly. The lack of any kind of clutch or gears meant that the motor could

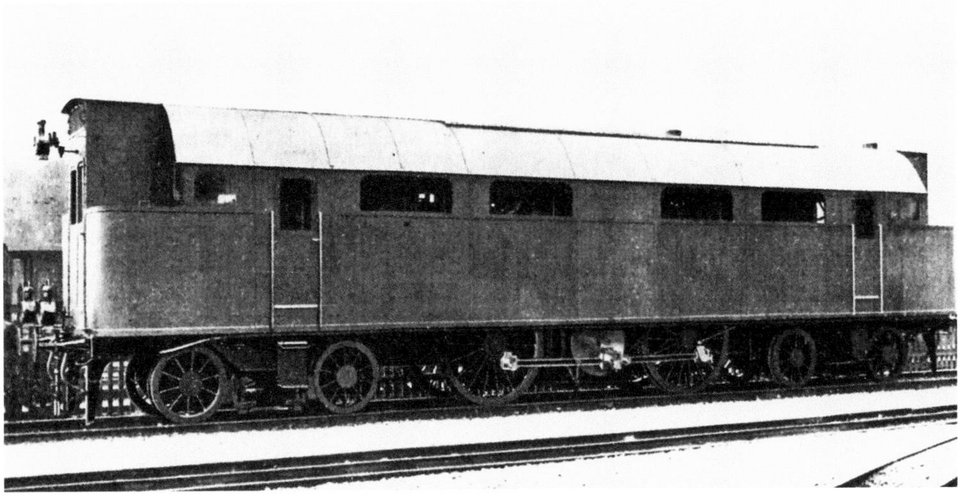

The first diesel locomotive.

not start the locomotive from stationary. In order to effect this a supplementary diesel engine, of 250 hp, drove a compressor feeding compressed air to the cylinders. Once a speed of 10 kph had been reached the main engine took over. The locomotive measured 16.6 metres, weighed 85 tonnes and had a top speed of 100 kph. Perhaps unsurprisingly the engine was not a great success and Sulzer subsequently went the way of four-stroke engines and electric transmission. The locomotive eventually found its way to the Prussian State Railway. Further development of diesel locomotives was held back by the First World War and it wasn't until the 1930s that diesels really came into their own for railway use.

On 29 September 1913, Diesel was on board the ship *Dresden*, sailing between Antwerp and Harwich, on his way to the AGM of one of the businesses with which he was involved. After dining with his companions, he retired for the night. In the morning no trace of him could be found. A week later a body was discovered by a Dutch ship and was identified as Diesel by the items in his pockets. The theories put forward for his death included murder, suicide and accident. As for the latter, it was speculated that Diesel may have fallen overboard during a night-time stroll, for he was a notorious insomniac. Suicide came to have greater credence when it was discovered, to everyone's surprise, that Diesel was on the verge of bankruptcy. He had £90,000 worth of debts and only £2,000 worth of assets. All his property was mortgaged. There was also a story that just before his trip he had given his wife a bag containing a large amount of cash, but warned her not to open it until a week had passed. The murder theory came about in the light of the increasing tensions between Britain and Germany and the imminence of war. Diesel was due to meet a British admiral while in England. Might the Germans have suspected that he was due to hand over some important secret that would not be available to them, and thus taken action to prevent this happening? We shall never know, but of one thing we can be certain: no inventor's name has ever been more firmly attached to his invention than that of Diesel.

Diesel Locomotives

Above left: These curious-looking machines were built in 1950–51 by the Société de Construction Ferroviaire et Navales at Sables d'Olonne. Some of the parts used were ex-US army surplus. They had two six-cylinder diesel engines, giving a total of 520 hp and a top speed of just 47 mph. Numbered DE-1–6, they were used on the Chemin de fer d'Herault network. When that closed in 1968 they were transferred to CFTA at Gray where they were used until the early 1990s. They had the nickname 'Mammouth'. DE-1 is seen in the yard at CFTA Gray.

Above right: This very large class of mixed traffic locomotives was built between 1969 and 1975. Once found all over the network, they are now in rapid decline, being replaced on passenger duties by various types of multiple unit, and on freight duties by newer types of locomotives. The class is equipped with a SEMT V16 engine, delivering 2,300 hp. No. 167441 is seen at St-Amand-Montrond in 2015.

Above left: When delivery started in 2006, these were the first new diesel locomotives built for SNCF in over thirty years. The class is a joint Siemens/Alstom design. Two different versions of the MTU 16 V 4000 engine are installed. No. 475405, seen here, is equipped with the more powerful version, which gives 3,200 hp.

Above right: At Auneau on 31 June 2014, Nos 460081 and 460144 wait for their next turn of duty. This class of locomotive, built by Alstom, was introduced in 2006. Power is provided by a 1,000-kW Caterpillar engine.

The Vossloh Euro 4000 diesel electric Co-Co is equipped with an EMD V16 two-stroke engine giving a power output of 4,300 hp. Europorte has thirty-two of these locomotives. In June 2012 No. 4003 stands at Gray waiting for its next turn of duty.

The G2000 BB was introduced by Vossloh in 2000. It has a 78-litre V16 3516B-HD Caterpillar engine, delivering 3,000 hp and a top speed of 75 mph. It has Voith hydraulic transmission and is designed for freight and heavy shunting use. This EuroCargo loco is seen at Port d'Atelier-Amance in 2009.

Now all withdrawn, except for a few machines kept for special duties, Class CC 72000 was SNCF's most powerful diesel. Built between 1967 and 1974, they were equipped with the SACM AGO V16ESHR engine, giving 3,500 hp and a top speed of 160 kph. Thirty machines were later equipped with the SEMT Pielstick V16 PA4 V200 VC engine and were renumbered in the CC 72100 series. On 14 September 2009, No. 72068, still in original livery, complete with *macaron*, stands at St-Germain-des-Fossés with a service for Paris.

E

Electric Locomotives

These locomotives were built in 1936/37 for the Etat electrification between Paris and Le Mans. They were based on the PO series 503–537, with which, mechanically, they were almost identical. Of the 2D2 type, they were rated at 4,100 hp and were originally limited to 100 kph – later raised to 140 kph. They were numbered in the 5400 series under SNCF. In this photograph by Ben Brooksbank we see No. 2D2 5409 taking over the St-Malo/Quiberon–Paris express at Le Mans on 17 October 1956.

The BB 88500 Class is a sub-class of the BB 8500 type. The members of the class have been downgraded to empty stock duties and have a maximum speed of 100 kph. Both types were built by Alsthom between 1964 and 1974. No. 88509 is seen at Paris Gare de Lyon on empty stock duty in October 2010.

Dating from 1969, Class CC 6500 was the most powerful on SNCF. These locomotives, which were equipped to operate on 1,500 V DC, had a power rating of 5,900 kW (7,900 hp) and a top speed of 200 kph. The whole class has now been withdrawn but several examples remain in preservation, including No. CC 6549, seen on display at Paris Gare de Lyon in December 2017. Behind is No. 2D2 9135. (Graham Skinner)

These two locomotives look to be identical and indeed have features in common. Both were built by Alsthom/MTE in the period 1976–86. Both are also equipped for push-pull working and have the same *nez-cassé* (broken-nose) design. There the similarities end, however, because while No. 507237 is equipped to operate exclusively on the 1,500-DC network, No. 522362 is a dual-voltage machine that can work on both the 1500-DC and 25-kV networks. They are seen at Beaune in 2016 while working Burgundy TER services between Paris and Lyon.

The SNCF Alstom Prima electric locomotive designed for freight haulage comes in a dual-voltage Class BB 27000 and a tri-voltage version – BB 37000. The Europorte version is Class BB 37500. Its maximum speed is 140 kph. BB 37505 is seen here on 17 July 2015.

English Electric

In 1992 a curious sight was seen in the hills of the Morvan, in central France. This was an English Electric diesel locomotive built some thirty years before for British Railways. The Class 20, a Bo-Bo diesel-electric with a V8, 1,000 hp engine, was one of the most successful designs of the BR Modernisation Plan. In 1992 four of these locomotives – Nos 20035, 20063, 20139 and 20228 – were purchased by the company Chemins de fer Départementaux. After modifications carried out by BREL Crewe, and renumbering as Nos 2001–2004, the machines were shipped out to France to start work between Montchanin, Etang-sur-Arroux and Cravant-Bazarnes. By 2002 all the machines were out of use, and in 2005 they were returned to the UK. Two of them survive to this day (2019): No. 20035 is at the Gloucestershire Warwickshire Railway and No. 20228 is at the Vale of Glamorgan Railway.

Nos 2001 and 2002 at Autun depot, mid-1990s.

Engerth

These Engerth locomotives were the first freight locomotives obtained by the Chemin de fer du Midi. No. 324, *la Maurouze*, was built by Kessler of Austria in 1856. The Engerth system involved the rear of the locomotive being carried on a sort of double Bissel truck, which allowed for greater mobility and adhesive weight. Although primarily intended for freight, their maximum speed of 65 kph allowed their use on passenger services as well. This was a very successful, long-lived class of locomotives and three of the type were still in use in 1938.

The Est and Alsace Lorraine Companies

The Chemin de fer de l'Est started out as the Chemin de fer de Paris à Strasbourg, founded in 1845. With the absorption of the Chemin de fer de Montereau à Troyes and the Chemin de fer de Blesme à Saint-Dizier the company changed its name to the Compagnie des Chemins de fer de l'Est. The Est continued to expand by extensions of its network and purchases of other companies until 1871. Following the Franco-Prussian War of 1870 and the annexation of Alsace-Lorraine, the railways of those regions were henceforth part of the German system. At the end of the First World War and the return of Alsace-Lorraine to France, the railways came under the control of the Administration des chemins de fer d'Alsace et Lorraine, which remained a separate entity until nationalisation in 1938. Both companies then became part of the SNCF.

Above left: These Est locomotives were extremely long-lived, being rebuilds of 0-6-0s dating back to the middle of the nineteenth century. Some of the class were rebuilt as two-cylinder simple engines while others were rebuilt as two-cylinder compounds. No. 130B 307 is one of the latter. It is seen at Chaumont in 1958. (Ben Brooksbank)

Above right: Est poster.

État

The Administration des Chemins de fer de l'État was created in 1878 by the French government to take over a number of failing lines in the area between the Loire and the Garonne. These lines amounted to some 2,600 km. In the 1980s an exchange was made with the PO to bring a more coherent shape to both networks. The État gave up the Saint-Nazaire–Croisic line and gained the Nantes–Sables-d'Olonne line. The takeover by the state did little to address the company's financial problems, nor did the absorption of the Compagnie des Chemins de fer de l'Ouest in 1908. In 1928 Raoul Dautry took over and set about putting the organisation in better shape. New, more comfortable carriages were ordered, a number of *autorails* were bought, and in 1937 the line from Paris to Le Mans was electrified. The following year the État became part of the nationalised network.

Above left: These *coupe-vent* 4-4-0s were built by Schneider in 1898. There were just four in the series. They were used on the Paris–Royan service, which included a nonstop run of 238 km. They were capable of speeds up to 125 kph.

Above right: No. 141C 14, seen at le Mans in 1956, dates from 1920 and was one of a class of 250 locomotives built for the État by Schneider. One of the class has survived into preservation. (Ben Brooksbank)

État poster.

F

Freight

After the Second World War SNCF decided to implement a new regime for the transport of freight. This was the system of *régime accéléré* (RA) and *régime ordinaire* (RO), which replaced the previously existing system of *grande vitesse* and *petite vitesse*. In Côte d'Or, in order to implement this new system, it was necessary to create a new *triage* for the RO traffic to supplement the yard at Dijon Perrigny, which thereafter would principally be dedicated to RA traffic.

This new yard would be at Gevrey-Chambertin, seen here. The yard at Gevrey was completed by 1952 and by 1962 was dealing with 3,500 wagons per day. The peak year for freight traffic in France was 1976. From that time on a slow decline began. In 1988, with the implementation of the *régime unique*, Perrigny no longer had a role as a marshalling yard. By 2006 Gevrey was handling just 1,400 wagons per day. In 2012 thirty-seven of the sorting sidings at Gevrey were handed over to Euro Cargo Rail, mainly for the purpose of the distribution of Peugeot and Citroën cars, on behalf of GEFCO.

The empty yard at Gevrey is symbolic of the decline of rail freight in France, which has been losing volume since the 1970s. Part of this loss is attributable to the arrival of private companies on the freight scene, but by far the majority of the loss has been to road transport. SNCF Fret has 4,700 employees and in 2017 carried 91 million tonnes of freight. This compares with 128 million tonnes just fifteen years previously.

In October 2014, *Sybic*, No. 26097, heads north through Chantenay-St-Imbert with a train of tanks. The name *Sybic* derives from the fact that these dual-voltage locomotives have synchronous motors. The 234 machines in the class have a maximum speed of 200 kph.

A pair of CFR Vossloh G1000 locomotives climb the freight-only, single-track line from Cercy-la-Tour to the quarry at Epiry-Montreuillon with a rake of empty *tremies*, which will be filled at the quarry. The photograph was taken in August 2013.

A pair of BB 67400 locomotives are seen near Verneuil on the Chagny–Nevers line, in September 2008, with a long train of sliding tarpaulin wagons.

On 25 September 2008 a pair of Class BB 66000 locos blast away from Etang-sur-Arroux with a train of timber from the forests of the Morvan. The design of these machines dates from 1959. Many have now been re-engined to become Class BB 69000.

At Negrondes in April 2013 a pair of Class BB 60000 engines approach the station with a trainload of limestone from the quarry at Thiviers Planeau.

G

Gares

In the early days of the railways in France there was some confusion about the name to give to places where the trains stopped. At Tours the first station was called an *embarcadère*, while at Troyes there was a *débarcadère*, rather implying that you could only get off there! *Station* was an early name, which somehow became *gare*, but really a *gare* was where you *garer* (park or keep) trains. Anyway, the name stuck and *gare* became universal. The Orange–Buis line (see page 52) had *gares*, *stations* and *haltes*. Some lines had *arrêts*.

Haltes were commonly found on metre-gauge minor lines and facilities were at an absolute minimum. A good example is seen at Villegaudin on the Chemins de fer d'intérêt local de Saône et Loire line between Chalons-sur-Saône and Mervans. This line opened in stages between 1901 and 1905 and closed completely in 1945. On the same line was the station of St-Marcel, very typical of stations on lines of *intérêt local*. On the right is the goods shed together with its loading platform and on the left are the 'conveniences'.

The *halte* of Villegaudin.

VIEUX TROYES. - L'ancien débarcadère de la première gare de TROYES inaugurée en 1847 et incendiée en 1855
(Ligne de TROYES à MONTEREAU)

Above left: The station of St-Marcel.

Above right: The *débarcadère* at Troyes.

In 1853 the Grand Central (GC) received the concession for a line, 'Montauban au Lot', conceived as part of a transversal Montauban to Clermont-Ferrand via Lexos, Capdenac, Figeac, Aurillac and Lempdes. In 1855 a further concession for a line from Capdenac to Brive was obtained, which was intended to form part of a transversal from Lyon to Bordeaux. By 1857 the GC was no longer viable as a company and its concessions were divided between the PLM and PO, the latter taking over the work already in hand on the Montauban line, which opened between Montauban and Capdenac in the summer of 1858. The original station at Capdenac burnt down in 1922 and its replacement (opened in 1928) caused some controversy, being in an unusual but nevertheless pleasing style, reflective of the local vernacular architecture.

The railway arrived in Strasbourg in 1841 and a permanent station was completed by 1852. Following the annexation of Alsace-Lorraine by Germany after the Franco-Prussian War of 1870, Strasbourg came under the authority of the Kaiserliche Generaldirektion der Eisenbahnen in Elsaß-Lothringen, which decided that a new station should be built. Work started in 1878 and was completed in 1883. This is the present station seen in the postcard view; however, in 2007 a vast glass verandah was built onto the façade. This structure stretches 125 metres has 900 panels of glass and weighs 650 tonnes.

Above left: The present station at Périgueux dates from the 1860s and is little changed from the view on the old postcard. It is at the meeting point of lines from Bordeaux, Limoges, Agen and Brive-la-Gaillarde and sees more than a million passengers a year.

Above right: The station at Vesoul opened in 1858 with the arrival of the line from Langres. This station of the Est company remains in original condition with the exception of the awning, which is a modern addition.

Béziers is an ex-Midi station on the line from Montpellier to Toulouse. It is also the southern terminus of the 'Aubrac', the much threatened electrified line from Neussargues. Dating from 1857, it is little changed and, unlike many other stations, retains its overall roof. It sees nearly 3 million passengers a year. The locomotive is a 4-6-0 of the 1301–1370 Class, dating from 1893. One of these locomotives has survived into preservation and can be found at the Cité du Train.

The Gare de l'Est in Paris was opened in 1849 by the Compagnie de Paris à Strasbourg and inaugurated the following year by the future Napoléon lll. The architect was François-Alexandre Duquesney. The station was originally named the Embarcadère de Strasbourg. Following the extension of the line to Mulhouse and the consequent renaming of the company as the Compagnie des Chemins de fer de l'Est, it was renamed Gare de l'Est. This view of the station is remarkably unchanged today, with the exception of the loss of a few chimney pots. The statue on top of the station represents the city of Strasbourg. The bus is a Line B service of the Compagnie générale des omnibus. Notice also the tram on the left and the Metro entrance on the right.

The stations of the Paris–Lyon railway were designed by Alexis Cendrier and are some of the most elegant in the whole of France, as here at Tournus. The station, which opened in 1854, is a good example of one of Cendrier's medium-sized stations and remains in remarkably original condition. In July 2015 a Paris–Lyon TER Bourgogne service arrives.

Montagne-sur-Sèvre on the closed line from St-Cristophe-du-Bois to Vouvant-Cézais is a typical country station. This line was first envisaged in 1879 but was only completed by the État company in 1914. The line went out of use progressively between 1960 and 1996. The station is now one of the two terminal stations of the preserved Chemin de fer de la Vendée.

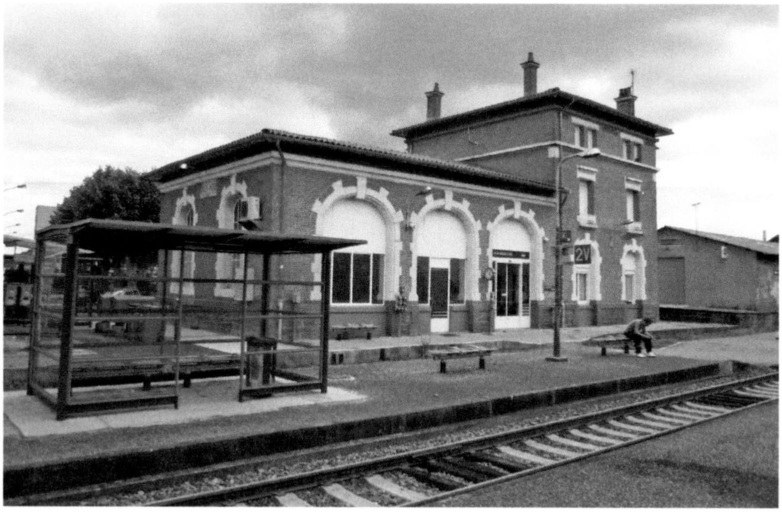

The station at Albi-Madeleine owes its origin to the Compagnie des houillères et Chemins de fer de Carmaux-Toulouse, which opened the line from Carmaux to Albi in 1858. In 1866 the line became part of the Midi network. In 1900 discussions started on a replacement for the existing timber station, but it was not until 1916 that the present building was finally opened. Albi is situated on the Toulouse–Rodez line and, as well as the local TER services, it also sees a sleeper service from Paris-Austerlitz at weekends.

Grosse C

10 LES LOCOMOTIVES FRANÇAISES (P.L.M.).
C127
P.L.M.
Machine C-127, Compound à vapeur saturée, 4 cylindres, tiroirs plans, 2 essieux accouplés et bogie, pour trains express. (Série C-61 à 180, construite en 1898-1902).
F. F. PARIS

The Grosse C 4-4-0s were constructed between 1898 and 1901. These machines, numbered C61-180 and also known as *coupes-vent* on account of their streamlining, were four-cylinder 4-4-0 saturated compounds, with 2-metre driving wheels (C101-120 1.98 m). Free-running machines, they were assigned to the fastest expresses. Speeds of up to 150 kph were recorded. The arrival of more powerful machines led to their relegation to less arduous duties. The name of Grosse C distinguished them from an earlier less powerful class of 4-4-0s numbered C21–60, which came to be known as Petites Cs.

H

Ligne des Hirondelles

From Champagnole in the *département* of Jura, situated at a height of 540 m, this line had to be constructed with a continuously rising gradient for 22 km, through forest and cuttings to St-Laurent-en-Grandvaux (920 m). Construction was slow, without mechanical assistance, and it was hardly possible to work on site during the long winters. The section from Champagnole to St-Laurent was opened in 1890. The biggest challenge for the engineers was still ahead of them. Ten more years would be needed to build the 13 km to Morez.

After St-Laurent, a tunnel of 2 km was built under the Col de la Savine. The line emerged at Morbier Gare at 860 m. The destination was Morez, located at the bottom of two narrow valleys where the Evalude River joins the Bienne at the north end of the town. It was concluded that the station at Morez should be created on a 'shelf' at 736 m on the east side of the Bienne valley, overlooking the town centre. Morez would be a terminus station and trains to St-Claude would reverse here. But how could the railway reach the site of the future station at Morez, which is 124 m lower than Morbier and only 3 km away in a straight line?

An audacious answer was found, and it became one of the rail wonders of France. The solution was to descend the west side of the Evalude valley, head upstream away from Morez to cross the river and, by means of a tunnel curving through 270 degrees, reach the east side of the valley to continue the descent into Morez station. The distance is 5.2 km along the single-track line between the two stations, with gradients of 1 in 25 and 1 in 30, four viaducts and three tunnels including the 270-degree Tunnel des Frasses. The station at Morbier was opened in May 1899 and the spectacular conclusion of the line at Morez was opened in June 1900. The whole line from Dole to St-Claude is promoted as the Ligne des Hirondelles, but undoubtedly the most spectacular part is the central section, described above.

The spectacular descent from Morbier to Morez: 1. Tunnel des Pâturages (66 m), 2. Viaduc Rom and 3. Viaduc des Crottes, 4. Viaduc de Morez, and 5. Viaduc de l'Evalude.

On 12 August 2014 diesel unit No. X 73567 has arrived at Morez from St-Claude. All trains reverse here, and the unit is ready to depart for Dole. It will soon be climbing up the Viaduc des Crottes, seen in the background.

I

Imperiale

Imperiale, in railway terms, has two meanings. It can refer to the line from Paris to Marseille or to double-deck carriages, an example of which is shown below. In 1864 the Compagnie du chemin de fer du Medoc ordered fifty passenger coaches, of which twenty were double-decked. These carriages were especially popular and survived into the twentieth century. They were all two-axled non-corridor coaches with heating by hot water bottles and lighting by oil lamps. Depending on the configuration they could seat between sixty-four and eighty-four.

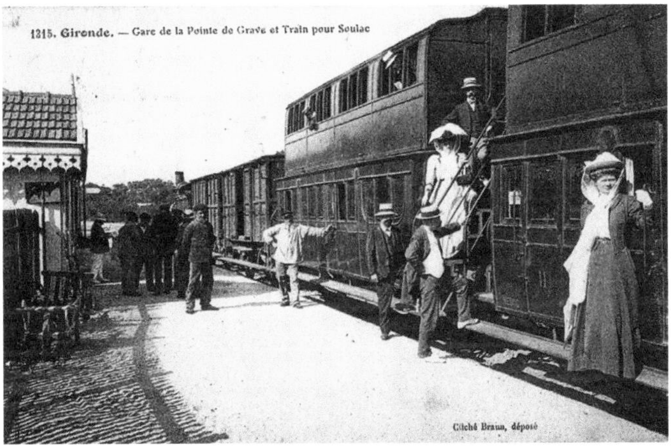
1315. Gironde. — Gare de la Pointe de Grave et Train pour Soulac
Cliché Braun, déposé

The Ligne Imperiale owes its name to nothing more than the fact that it was used by the Emperor Napoleon III. The construction of the first section of the line is described here. The first proposal for a line from Paris to Lyon was put forward by M. Blum in March 1932. In May of that same year a further proposal was made by M. M. Mellet and Henry. Their route was what eventually became the Bourbonnais line, which travelled via Nevers, Moulins and Roanne to St-Etienne, where it would join the already existing line to Lyon. The following year M. M. Desfontaines and Arnollet suggested a route following the path of the Seine, serving Troyes and Châtillon-sur-Seine and proceeding via Til-Châtel to Dijon. In August 1838 Hyacinthe Bruchet suggested a route via Corbeil, Montereau, Pont-sur-Yonne, Saulieu and Epinac to Chagny. The line suggested by M. Courtois would have passed far to the east, via Arcis-sur-Aube, Bar-sur-Aube, Til-Châtel and Dijon. Yet another route was suggested by a M.Polonçeau: similar to the Bruchet route as far as Joigny, it then followed the Canal de Bourgogne and the valley of the Ouche to Dijon.

Following the passing of the Loi Legrand in 1842, the choice of route was narrowed down to three: those of Arnollet, Polonçeau and Bruchet. The president of Ponts et Chaussées declared that he was in favour of the latter. It will be noted that this route did not pass via Dijon, which would have been served by a branch. From Chagny the main line would have passed via Chalon and the valley of the Saône to Lyon. Not unnaturally, the Dijonnais were not at all happy about the decision and a native of Dijon, Henry Darcy, set about investigating a route that would take the line via Dijon. The problem for all the lines was getting across or through the range of hills to the north-west of Dijon known as le Seuil de Bourgogne. Darcy's proposal included a 3,700-metre tunnel at Blaisy-Bas (in reality 4,100 m) and in doing so took a more direct route to Dijon. Darcy now had to convince parliament to approve his route, which he succeeded in doing – the law of 7 July 1845 was the result. Work between Paris and Tonnerre, and between Dijon and Chalon, led to the opening of these two lines in 1849.

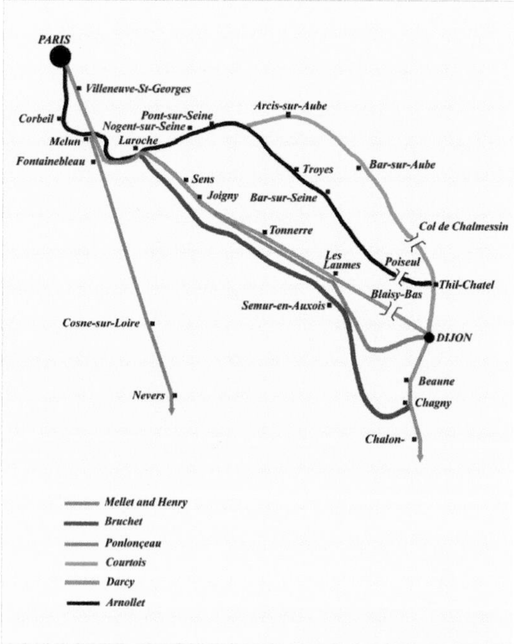

The various routes proposed for the Paris–Lyon line.

Le Seuil de Bourgogne causes little trouble these days for a 4,040-kW electric locomotive. No. 507240 climbs the gradient leading to the tunnel of Blaisy-Bas on 11 September 2015 with a Paris Bercy–Lyon service.

J

Jacquemin

André Jacquemin worked for the Paris-Orléans company and then in the Division des études de la traction électrique of SNCF, where he was responsible for the design of the mechanical parts of electric locomotives, including the record-breaking BB 9004. He subsequently designed the mechanical parts of a number of similar-looking locomotives, which popularly became known as 'Jacquemins'. These classes included BB 25200. BB 25236, restored to original livery, is seen at Dijon at the head of a special from Paris on 18 September 1999. The special was to commemorate the 50th anniversary of the electrification 1,500 V DC from Paris–Dijon. Class BB 25200 were dual-voltage locomotives introduced in 1969 – now all withdrawn. (Graham Skinner)

K

Koechlin

André Koechlin became interested in steam locomotion through his involvement in the textile industry. In 1839 he constructed his first locomotive, later named *Napoléon*. The Koechlin company remained one of the leading locomotive manufacturers and eventually merged with Elsässische Maschinenbau-Gesellschaft Grafenstaden in 1872, when the company became Société Alsacienne de Constructions Mécaniques.

One of Koechlin's locomotives, *Ceinture No. 3*, works No. 1247, built 1870, became Nord 040T No. 4963.

L

La Machine

One of the earliest railway lines in France was at La Machine in the *département* of Nièvre. This curious name was the result of the eighteenth-century installation of a machine designed by a Belgian engineer, Daniel Michel. This horse-powered engine was used to haul coal to the surface. Its novelty caused it to become something of a celebrity and the machine eventually gave its name to the locality. The price of coal was directly related to the cost of transportation. In the early nineteenth century the coal mined at La Machine was transported to the Loire at Decize by horse-drawn wagons, which was still the case in 1838, and thoughts now turned towards the construction of a railway. Two routes were considered: via the valley of La Meule and via the valley of Fondjudas. The first would have led directly to the Loire; the second to the Canal du Nivernais. It was the second that won the day. Work started in 1841 and was completed by 1843. The gauge was 110 cm and haulage was by horses. At the same time, lines were constructed within the mine complex. These included two inclined planes. Much of the intra-mine network was of a gauge of 50 cm.

In 1869 the mines became part of the Schneider empire and, with production reaching 1,000 tonnes per day, improvements were needed to the transport system. In 1868 a branch was opened from the PLM Nevers–Chagny line at Decize to the Port de la Copine (the point of discharge for the wagons from La Machine), enabling the transport of coal by railway as well as by canal and river. In 1875 work was started on rebuilding the railway line of Fondjudas to standard gauge. Work was completed in 1877. Two 0-6-0 and two 0-4-0 tanks were provided by Schneider for the standard-gauge line, and two 0-4-0s for the 50-cm-gauge lines.

In 1955 the internal rail network was removed in favour of lorry transport, and in 1965 steam traction ended on the Fondjudas line. Coal production ceased in 1974. The former offices of the mine have been turned into a museum. The headworks and part of one of the mines have been retained, and a trip underground is included in the museum visit. The Fondjudas line has been made into a very pleasant path for walking or cycling. The Port de la Copine still exists but is now used exclusively for pleasure craft.

One of the 50-cm-gauge locomotives at work at the Marguerite mine.

Library

An interesting building of the Schneider empire at Le Creusot that survived the demolitions of the 1980s is the loco-erecting shop. Built in 1850, it was used for the purpose its name suggests until 1950 when it became a warehouse. In 1975 it was classified as a *monument historique* and in 1998 it was converted to become the library for the Centre Universitaire Condorcet. This change of use involved a remarkable piece of conservation. Not only have the girders upon which the travelling cranes used to run been kept, but so also have three of the cranes themselves.

The erecting shop at Le Creusot with a pair of 4-6-0s under construction.

The erecting shop turned into a library. The overhead cranes are still there.

Limoges

Limoges is on the electrified line from Paris to Toulouse – the so-called 'POLT' line. It is an important junction and, as well as the main line, there are lines to Clermont-Ferrand, Périgueux, Angoulême and Poitiers. The first station, constructed of timber, was opened in 1856. The present station dates from 1929 and was designed by Roger Gonthier. It is unusual in being built on a raft above the platforms. It sees the passage of 1.6 million passengers per year.

This photograph was taken in 1956. On the right a Unifié 600 hp *autorail* can be seen. (Ben Brooksbank)

M

La Malle des Indes

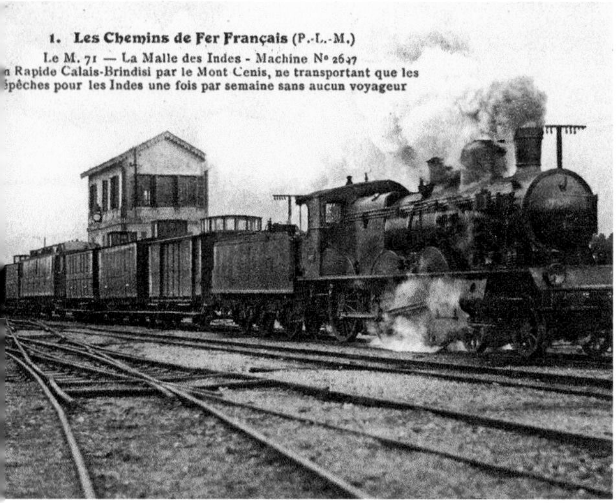
1. Les Chemins de Fer Français (P.-L.-M.)
Le M. 71 — La Malle des Indes - Machine N°
Rapide Calais-Brindisi par le Mont Cenis, ne transportant que les
pêches pour les Indes une fois par semaine sans aucun voyageur

La Malle des Indes was the name of a train that transported mail across France on its journey from Britain to India. Starting in the 1830s, this mail had been carried by various means across France before continuing its journey by ship. From 1856 the transit through France from the Channel ports to Marseille was entirely by train. In 1871 the destination became Brindisi. This is the era depicted in the photograph. The service continued until 1930, after which air transport took over. The locomotive is a four-cylinder compound, one of a class of ten machines introduced in 1909.

Mallet

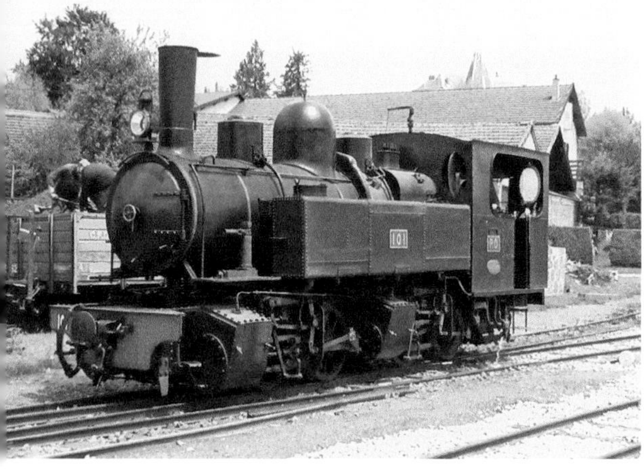

The Mallet system consisted of a combination of articulation and compounding. This would give both flexibility – the Mallet system was often used on metre-gauge systems – and economy. Mallet's design had the high-pressure cylinders on the main frame with the low-pressure cylinders on the forward, articulating, Bissell truck. The PO metre-gauge Correze system had four 0-4-0+0-4-0 Mallets, numbered 101 to 104, constructed by Blanc-Misseron. No. 101 was in use from 1906 to 1969. It has been preserved and is seen here at Tence on the Voies Ferrées du Velay. Nos 103 and 104 have also been preserved.

Midi

The Chemin de fer du Midi was set up by the Pereire brothers in 1852. It completed its first line from Bordeaux to Dax in 1854. It continued to develop its network in the far south-west of France such that at its amalgamation with the PO in 1934 it had a network of 4,313 km. The Midi was an early adopter of electrification, and to this end it constructed a number of hydro-electric power stations in the Pyrenees. By the time of its amalgamation all its principal lines were electrified.

This four-cylinder compound of the series 1301–1370 was constructed between 1896 and 1910. It was an extremely successful type. It became SNCF 230B 601–670 and the last was withdrawn in 1959. One has survived into preservation.

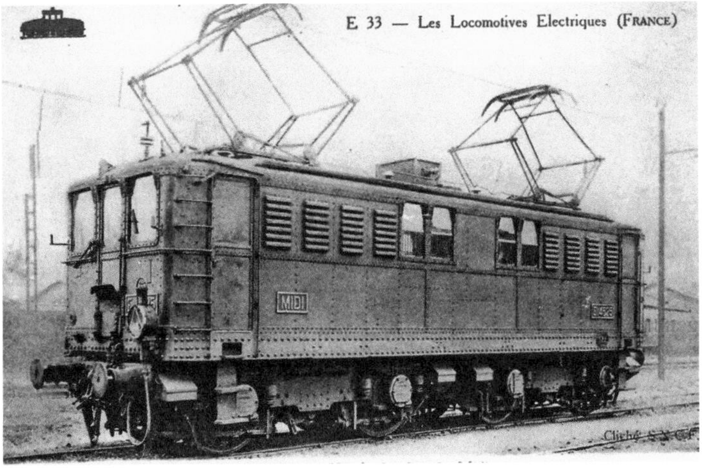

This series of fifty locomotives was constructed between 1923 and 1926. With a power rating of 1,100 hp and a top speed of 90 kph these machines were intended for light mixed-traffic use. Under SNCF they became BB 1601–1650. The last was withdrawn in 1984. One is preserved at the Cité du Train. All the Midi electric locomotives had this same box-like shape.

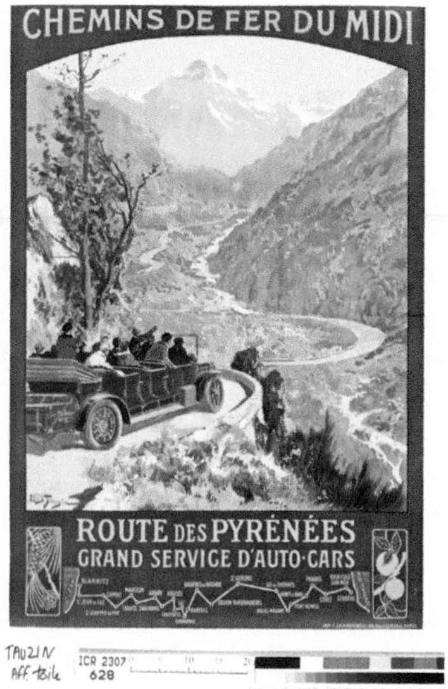

Midi poster.

Misty Mistral

Not in fact the *Mistral* but a special train at Cercy-la-Tour hauled by the preserved No. 141R 1199. This locomotive was built for SNCF by Baldwin in 1947 and was one of the 1,323 machines of this class supplied by American engine manufacturers. Twelve have been preserved. The *Mistral* train was introduced by SNCF in 1950 to run between Paris and Marseille. From 1952 it was extended to Nice. In 1964 journey time was 10 hours 21 minutes, which made it one of the fastest trains in France. The average speed between Paris and Dijon was 132.8 kilometres per hour. During the period of steam haulage, the *Mistral* was often hauled by a 141R. In 1965 electric traction took over. The train ceased running in 1982.

N

North British Locomotive Company

In 1913 seventy of these locomotives were built by three French constructors for the État network. During the First World War a further 200 locomotives were ordered from two British companies: the North British Locomotive Co. and Naysmith Wilson & Co. These machines were delivered in 1916 and 1917. The French rail-mounted heavy artillery, the Artillerie Lourde sur Voie Ferrée, ordered a further seventy engines, with half being built by NBL and the other half by the Vulcan Foundry. These locomotives were extremely long-lived. A number were hired out to the CFTA at Gray and became the last steam locomotives active on the French network. Eight have survived into preservation. The engine pictured here, No. 140C 188, is seen at Sommesous on the freight-only line between Chalons and Troyes on 23 September 1958. It is one of the NBL-built examples. (Ben Brooksbank).

Narrow Gauge

In the period before the First World War there were more than 20,000 km of minor railways in France. This was in addition to the main railway companies. Most of these lines were metre-gauge although there were some exceptions. Almost every *département* had a network of these lines. Some *départements* had several. The majority of these railways were built in the period 1880 to 1914. After the First World War the decline started, mainly due to competition from road transport. This decline continued through the 1930s but was arrested to some extent during the Second World War due to the scarcity of fuel for road vehicles. Today nearly all have gone, and it is difficult to believe that this vast network once existed. Surviving metre-gauge lines include the Blanc-Argent and the Chemin de fer de Provence. There are also a number of lines that have survived as tourist railways. Notable among these are the Chemin de fer du Vivarais and the Baie de Somme network. Below is the story of one railway that did not survive – the Chemins de fer Vicinaux de Haute Saône. It typifies many others that went the same way (see also Tramways de l'Ardèche, page 8).

In 1873 a company was formed to build a line from Gray to Bucey-les-Gy. The *declaration d'utilité publique* was received in 1874 and the line was completed and opened by May 1878. The Compagnie du Chemin de Fer de Gray à Gy et Prolongements (CFGGP) was unfortunately unable to live up to its name, since it was able neither to prolong its line nor its existence. Financial problems led to its failure, and the line already built was incorporated into the concession granted to the Compagnie Générale des Chemins de fer Vicinaux. The *conseil général* of Haute Saône wished to extend the network and new lines were opened from Gy to Marnay (1894), Ronchamp to Plancher-les-Mines (1895), Bucey-les-Gy to Frétigny (1899) and Gray to Dole (1901). This constituted the first network, and almost immediately it was decided to build a second network, which opened as follows: Luxeil–Coravillers (1902), Gray–Jussey, Lure–Ronchamp, Lure–Le Haut-de-Them (1903) and Lure–Hericourt (1904).

In 1907 a third network was decided on in order to connect parts of the network isolated from the rest, as well as to build new lines. These lines were: Vesoul–Molay (1910), Fretigny–Grandvelle–Vesoul, Grandvelle–Besançon, Vesoul–Luxeil, Courcelle–Vauvillers, Vesoul–St-Georges (1911) and Le Haut-de-Them–Le Thillot (1912). This gave a grand total of 529 km of lines, upon which there were 245 *gares, haltes* and *arrêts*. The *conseil général* planned a fourth network of a further 170 km of lines, but the First World War intervened before this work could be carried out.

The lines were built as far as possible along roadsides, this being the case more so for the earlier lines than the later. The major works were kept to a minimum but inevitably on such an extensive network there was a large number of bridges and several substantial viaducts and cuttings. The most significant work was the tunnel under the Col des Croix, on the line to Le Thillot. This 1,097-metre-long tunnel took three years to build, finally opening in November 1912. Station buildings were for the most part rudimentary, consisting of just a single-storey waiting room and office, with a goods shed attached at one side. There was no accommodation for staff. One consequence of this minimalist design is that, unlike elsewhere, few of the stations have been utilised as dwellings and many remain in original condition – often abandoned. As the network grew, some of the junction stations received new or extended buildings. The headquarters of the company was at Vesoul, and there were workshops at Vesoul, Lure and Gray.

The CFV inherited a number of locomotives from the ephemeral CFGGP, including three SACM 0-6-2 tanks (Nos 1–3) and a Fives-Lille 0-6-0 (No. 4). A Corpet-Louvet 0-6-0 was purchased in 1890 and in 1898 six Weidknecht 0-4-2s of 16 tonnes were received and numbered 5–10. The original locomotives had twin buffers, but at this time the CFV decided to standardise on the single central buffer. The earlier machines and rolling stock were adapted accordingly. In 1901 three Pinguely 0-6-0 *bicabines* were purchased and were given the numbers 3, 11 and 12. The front cabin was soon removed. For the second network, thirteen Pinguely 0-6-0s of 18 tonnes were ordered. They were allocated spare numbers between 1 and 12, and 13 to 16. This must have been very confusing for workshop staff. For the third network a total of fifteen Corpet-Louvet 0-6-0s were received, being given the more logical number sequence of 31 to 45. During the First World War a number of Baldwin 0-6-2s were used on military traffic. Passenger rolling stock consisted of a mixture of bogied and two-axled vehicles, the majority being of the end-platform type. Altogether there were more than a hundred passenger carriages and *fourgons*. Goods vehicles amounted to a total of 573 of all the usual types.

All lines, bar one, had the familiar three returns per day, with additional trains on fair days on some lines. The exception was the Lure–Le Thillot line, which enjoyed four return services per day. Goods traffic was considerable, and there were no less than seventy-five private branches, the majority of these being near Gray or in the east of the *département*. Traffic was particularly heavy during the First World War, when much material needed at the front was carried, especially on the Lure–Le Thillot line. Passenger services were reduced to two per day during the conflict, a situation continuing thereafter, although supplemented by additional trains on fair and market days.

As elsewhere in France, the prosperity of the pre-war days had gone forever. Through the 1920s costs increased, receipts fell and the deficit grew. In 1928 the *conseil général* decided to invest in a fleet of *autorails*, and in 1930 took receipt of seven De Dion-Bouton *autorails* type JM3 (Nos VA 1–7), and five trailers type KX (Nos VR 1–5). They were used on all lines except Vesoul–Hericourt, Lure–St-Georges, Comb–Molay and Lure–Plancher-les-Mines. The usual pattern of service on the remaining lines was for one service to be in the hands of an *autorail*, with the other(s) steam hauled. The timetable for 1933 shows that services between Gy and Marnay, and Vauvillers and Courcelles were given over entirely to *autorails*. Apart from these, there were seven other journeys each day employing *autorails*, the rest remaining steam hauled. Where the *autorails* were used there were considerable savings in journey times – as much as an hour in the case of Gray–Jussey.

The advent of the *autorails* made little difference to the financial state of the company, and in 1937 the *département* took over running of the network with the aim of transferring traffic to road. Between 1937 and 1938 the network gradually closed down and the lines were declassified in 1939. Track lifting started the same year. As well as the station buildings mentioned above, nearly all of which remain in existence, many in original condition, there are numerous other traces of the CFV, including bridges, viaducts and cuttings. The headquarters building of the company at Vesoul still stands as do the workshops at Gray. For those interested in railway archaeology the area is well worth a visit.

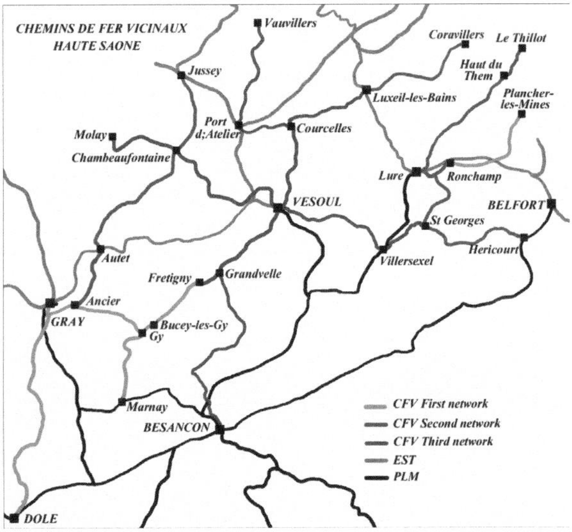

This map of the CFV network shows how extensive it once was.

216 - CORRAVILLERS (Hte-Saône) - La Gare
David, Luxeuil

A Corpet-Louvet runs round its train at the terminal station of Corravillers.

Apremont, delightfully preserved and typical of many of the stations on the network.

Although almost all these metre-gauge lines have been lost a good deal of material still survives. Some examples are shown in the accompanying photographs.

Owned by the Musée des Tramways à Vapeur et des Chemins de fer Secondaires français (MTVS) is this unique Brissoneau et Lotz diesel-electric *locotracteur*, which dates from 1937. It is built on the chassis of a steam engine. In 2001 it was classified as a *monument historique*. It is seen at the MTVS base at Butry-sur-Oise.

This is De Dion Bouton JM4 *autorail* No. 11, built in 1932 for the metre-gauge network in the *département* of Côtes du Nord in Brittany. The network had nineteen lines totalling 452 km. The first line opened in 1905 and the last closed in 1956.

The 0-3-0T steam tram comes from the Compagnie des Tramways de la Sarthe, a network around Le Mans. In 2018, the tram No. 60, *La Ferté Bernard*, celebrated its 120th birthday. It was built in 1898 by the Ateliers de construction du Nord de la France at Blanc Misseron. It is owned and operated by MTVS. In the background is Côtes-du-Nord Corpet-Louvet 0-6-0T No. 36.

Billard was a prominent builder of metre-gauge *autorails*. Automotrice A 150D2 No. 222 was built for the Vivarais network in 1939. In July 2014 it stands at St-Agrève on the preserved Velay-Express network.

At the base of Le Petit Anjou at St-Jean-de-Linières is Pinguely 0-6-0T No. 16, originally of the Chemin de fer de la Drôme. It was built in 1899 and is a *monument historique*. It is currently awaiting a new boiler. Next to it is a Billard *draisine*.

Nord

The Compagnie du chemin de fer du Nord was founded in 1845 and granted the concession to build a line from Paris to the Belgian border via Lille and Valenciennes, with branches to Calais and Dunquerke. Rapid expansion by the absorption of other companies led to the Nord having one of the largest and densest networks in France. One of the most outstanding chief motive power engineers of the Nord was Gaston du Bousquet, who was in post from 1890 to 1910.

In 1905, du Bousquet designed a locomotive based on the Meyer-Kitson system. This was a 0-6-2+2-6-0T 4-cylinder compound articulated locomotive. The boiler, firebox and cab assembly was supported on two pivoting trucks. The forward truck carried the low-pressure cylinders, and the rear the high pressure. The Nord built a total of forty-eight of these engines. The Est Company and the Syndicat des Chemins de fer de Ceinture de Paris purchased machines to the same design. The last was withdrawn from SNCF service in 1952.

One of du Bousquet's more conventional designs was the 4-6-0 of the series 3.513–3662 (SNCF 230D). These 149 locomotives were constructed between 1908 and 1912 and the last remained in service until 1969. Two are preserved: 230D 9 at the Cité du Train at Mulhouse, and 230D 116 at AJECTA Longueville. The latter machine was brought to England in the 1970s and spent some time on the Nene Valley Railway. It was eventually repatriated to France in 2009 with the help of funds raised by the SNCF Society (now the French Railways Society). It has not steamed since its return to France. In 1956 one of the class, 230D 124, stands at Abbeville with a local service. (Ben Brooksbank)

O

Orange to Buis

The line Orange–Buis-les-Baronnies is remarkable in that the discussions that led to its opening lasted just about as long as it was in operation. It was also unusual as the concession was awarded to the PLM and the line was classed as of *intèrêt général*. First discussions took place in 1860 when various routes were looked at. Other discussions followed, but nothing came of any of this. Given new impetus by the 'plan Freycinet', a study was approved for the Orange–Vaison-la-Romaine line. Discussions continued, with various modifications and alternative schemes being put forward. Finally, on 23 April 1889, an agreement was signed between the prefects of the *départements* of Drôme and Vaucluse for the construction of a line from Orange to Buis, with a branch to Carpentras via Malucéne. The contract for construction was awarded to the Compagnie des tramways du Buis de Rolland & Bonfils. However, nothing happened, and the aforesaid company was dissolved in March 1890.

In April 1892 the Compagnie des chemins de fer de la Drôme, together with the PLM, applied for a concession for a line of metre gauge between Orange and Buis. On 10 August 1893 the concession was awarded to the PLM and the section Orange–Vaison was declared of *utilité publique*. A further three years were to pass before the section Vaison–Buis was also declared of *utilité publique*. But that was not the end of the matter as arguments continued about the siting of stations. The definitive scheme received ministerial approval in 1902, but work to build the line did not start until 1905. Work was finished by 1907 and the inaugural train ran on 29 April 1907. Regular services began on 10 May.

The exploitation of the line was carried out by the Société Générale des Chemins de Fer Economiques (SE) on behalf of the PLM. There were two return services per day, soon augmented by a third, with all trains being mixed. Journey time on the ascent to Buis was around 2 hours 40 minutes, giving an average speed of just under 19 kph; and on the descent to Orange around 2 hours 20 minutes, making an average of just over 21 kph. Motive power was provided by five Corpet-Louvet 2-6-0 tanks numbered 3995–3999. There were ten 1st/2nd bogie carriages manufactured by Decauville, and a number of *fourgons* of both two-axle and bogie types. Some of these *fourgons* were equipped with a postal compartment, allowing sorting and franking en route. There were fifty-eight freight wagons of various types provided by SA Petolat. In the years immediately before the First World War the increase in traffic led to the acquisition of further rolling stock, including two 2-6-0 tanks from Decauville. These were numbered 3993/4. At the same time a *facultative* freight train was instituted between Orange and Vaison.

As with so many other secondary lines, the advent of the First World War had a drastic effect on the line, and services were reduced to one return trip per day. However, with the return of peace came the return of traffic and a second boom period. There were three mixed return services per day, plus a train just for freight. By 1930 there was an additional daily passenger service between Orange and Vaison. The boom did not last. As elsewhere, the rise in road transport in the 1930s led to a rapid decline in traffic – both passenger and freight. In October 1938, shortly after the creation of SNCF, of which the line was now part, the passenger service was replaced by road cars. The freight service continued with two round trips per day.

At the outbreak of the Second World War all services on the line were suspended, restarting with some difficulty after the signing of the armistice in 1940. Shortage of fuel for road transport led to the reinstatement of passenger services by the addition of a carriage to the freight trains. In August 1944 the service was reduced to a shuttle between Orange and Violès, to serve the nearby German air base. Elsewhere the line had been breached by the actions of the *maquis*. All services came to a stop on 22 August following the machine-gunning by an Allied aircraft of a train in the station at Orange.

After the war service resumed, but with only one mixed train per day. The writing seemed to be on the wall for the line, and the SE proposed the purchase of more modern material – specifically diesel *autorails* and *locotracteurs*. On 22 September 1948 the closure of the line was formally announced. A committee of defence and modernisation was set up in 1949. This committee must have had some clout, as well as friends in high places. None other than Édouard Daladier, president of the Republic, rose in defence of the line. There were meetings with ministers, deputies and officials of SNCF over the next few years. Even Paris Match joined in the bid to save the line, with a four-page pictorial feature in the edition of 8 November 1952. All this, nevertheless, came to nothing and the last train ran on 15 December 1952.

One of the Corpet-Louvet locomotives waits to leave Buis-les-Baronnies.

Gare d'Orsay

152 PARIS. — Intérieur de la Nouvelle Gare d'Orléans. - LL.

The Gare d'Orsay was completed in 1900 to the design of Victor Laloux. This gave the PO a location for its terminus nearer the centre of Paris than was the case with the Gare d'Austerlitz. A new 3.8-km line, mostly in tunnel, was constructed to connect the two stations. It was felt to be impractical to use steam haulage through the tunnel, so the lines were electrified at 650 V third rail. To haul the trains between the two stations the PO purchased eight 1,100 hp Bo-Bo locomotives from Thomson Houston. These were numbered E1 to E8. Their centre cab appearance caused them to be given the nickname 'boites de sel'. One of these machines can be seen in the photograph.

The increasing length of PO trains eventually made the Gare d'Orsay impractical as its platforms could not be extended, and from 1939 long-distance trains reverted to terminating at Gare d'Austerlitz. After the Second World War the station had various uses until it was decided to convert it into a museum for works of art of the later part of the nineteenth century. The Musée d'Orsay opened in 1983.

P

Pas Perdus

Enthused by the law of 1842, initiating the idea of a national network of railway lines, in 1844 the *Troyens* set up the Société Anonyme du Chemin de Fer Montereau à Troyes. They had hoped that the new Paris–Lyon line would pass through their city but it was not to be, and thus a line connecting Troyes with the PL at Montereau was conceived. The line opened in April 1848, but it was to be another fifteen months before the citizens of Troyes would be able to travel to Paris, with the section of the PL line to Tonnerre only being completed in August 1849. The station at Troyes, known as the '*débarcadére*', was constructed as a terminus. It was completed in time for the opening but burnt down in February 1855. A new through station was built on a different site and opened in time for the start of the service from Paris through to Mulhouse in 1858. Between 1892 and 1894 the station was enlarged and a 132-metre-long *marquise* was built over the platforms. In 1912 the beautiful, neo-classical *salle de pas perdus* seen here was added. This curious name derives from the pacing, backwards and forwards, often encountered in such a waiting area.

PLM

The Chemin de fer de Paris à Lyon et à la Méditerranée (PLM) could trace its origins back to the first railway built in France, and indeed in the whole of Continental Europe. This was the 18-kilometre-long line between Saint-Etienne and Andrezieux, constructed by the Chemin de fer de Saint-Etienne à la Loire, which opened in 1827 (see page 68). Other lines soon followed and were amalgamated into the Chemin de fer de junction du Rhône à la Loire. The big moment in the development of the PLM came in 1957 with the merger of the Chemin de fer de Paris à Lyon and the Chemin de fer de Lyon à la la Méditerranée, together with the absorption of the Chemin de fer de Lyon à Genève, and part of the Grand-Central. The new PLM continued to expand so that by 1909 its trains ran over 3,000 km of track. In that year it owned 3,000 locomotives, 6,600 carriages and 96,775 wagons, making it the largest of the pre-nationalisation companies. In 1938 the Société National de Chemin de Fer was created and the PLM became the south-eastern division of the state railway.

This very large class of nearly 300 locomotives was introduced in 1907. Like all PLM engines built since 1888 it was a four-cylinder compound. With its 5-foot driving wheels it was intended for heavy freight work. The maximum speed was 85 kph.

PLM poster.

PLM Pacifics

The story of the PLM Pacifics is a complex one. In 1909 two machines were produced: No. 6001 was a four-cylinder, saturated, compound with 2-metre driving wheels (as had all subsequent PLM Pacifics); No. 6101 was a four-cylinder, simple, superheated machine. Extensive trials were carried out to compare the two machines, which showed No. 6101 to be the better engine, in terms of fuel economy and water consumption. As a result of this, No. 6001 was given a superheater in 1912. Under the PLM renumbering it became 231C 1. Although, as the very first Pacific built by the PLM, this engine might have seemed suitable for preservation, in fact it was scrapped without ceremony in 1947.

No. 6001 in original form.

No. 6101 in original form.

A further seventy locomotives of the 6101 type were built in 1911–12. They received the numbers 6102–6171, subsequently 231A 1–71. A further twenty, Nos 6171–6191, were built in 1912, but these had a boiler with a pressure of 200 psi, as opposed to the 170 psi of the first series. Also in 1912, the PLM received twenty superheated compounds, with boilers at 227 psi. These were numbered 6011–6030 (later 231C 2–86). Comparisons between this latter series of compounds and the 6172–6191 simple engines showed an economy of 12 per cent in favour of the former. As a result of this, between 1917 and 1924 all of the 6172–6191 series were converted to compounds, after which they were renumbered 6051–6070, and then 231B 1–20. Between 1925 and 1930 it was the turn of the 170 psi series, 6102–6171, to be rebuilt as compound machines. They became 231E 1–71.

Between 1921 and 1925 a further series of 230 Pacifics were built. Yet more four-cylinder compounds, these had a boiler identical to the very first Pacific, No. 6001, except for the increase in pressure to 227 psi. The machines built up to 1922 were numbered 6301–6480, and subsequently 231D 1–180. The last batch of fifty, built in 1925, received the numbers 231D 181–230.

In 1929, 231D 141 was rebuilt with a new, higher pressure boiler (284 psi as opposed to the previous 227 psi), new cylinders with enlarged passages, a new blast pipe, a feed water heater and various other modifications. It was first renumbered 231F 141, then 231H 141, and finally, under the auspices of the SNCF, 231H 1. Between 1940 and 1948 the SNCF converted a further twenty-nine locomotives to the same specification, forming Class 231H 1–30. Twelve of the conversions were of the 231B type, and seventeen of the 231E type. The remaining eight unrebuilt 231Bs were withdrawn in 1947, with the unrebuilt 231Es following suit by 1952. 231H 21 was the last survivor of its class, being withdrawn from Nevers depot in 1966.

The final series of Pacifics built by the PLM appeared in 1931/1932. These fifty-five locomotives took the numbers 231F 231–285. These machines were essentially the same as the 231D Class. Twenty of the latter were rebuilt with feed water heaters and renumbered in the 231F Class. They kept their original series number, merely changing the D to F. They formed the series 231F 2–166.

In 1934, 231D 21 was rebuilt as 231G 21. It received a new blastpipe, new cylinders with enlarged passages, a higher degree of superheat, and other changes. Between 1934 and 1936 the whole of the class 231F 231–285 and some of the 231D class were rebuilt to become 231G 2–285. The process of rebuilding the 231Ds continued under the SNCF and by 1949 a total of 160 rebuilds had been completed. The remaining unrebuilt machines only survived until the mid-1950s. The series 231F 2–166 were also converted by the PLM to become 231G, a process completed by the SNCF. The last operational member of the class, 231G 64, was withdrawn from service at Nevers in 1966.

Another rebuild in 1934 was of 231C 9 (previously 6019, then 6209) in a manner similar to the conversions of classes 231D+F into 231G. In 1938 this engine was renumbered by the SNCF as 231K 9. A further eighty-four of the series 231C were rebuilt to form the series 231K. The last two of these in service were 231K 8 and 82. Both have been preserved.

In 1933, 231C 17 was another engine subject to a rebuild. Many aspects were similar to previous rebuilds, with one important difference. This was the fitting of Lentz oscillating cam valves. The locomotive was first renumbered 231I 17, then 231K 17, despite being unlike the other members of that class. In 1946 it was rebuilt to the same specification as the 231G type, but retained its number as 231K 17.

No. 231F 152, a rebuild from the 231D series.

On 23 September 1958 PLM Pacific No. 231K 70 heads away from Chalons-sur-Marne with a Paris–Strasbourg express. (Ben Brooksbank)

PO

The company was founded on 13 August 1838 under the name Compagnie du chemin de fer de Paris à Orléans (PO) and was awarded the concession to build a line from Paris to Orléans. The line was opened on 2 May 1843. At 114 kilometres, it was then the longest railway line in France. In the following years it absorbed a number of other companies. These included the Compagnie du chemin de fer de Tours à Nantes and the Compagnie du chemin de fer d'Orléans à Bordeaux. By 1912 it operated over a network of 7,790 km. In 1934 the PO merged with the Chemin du fer du Midi, giving the joint company a network of 12,000 km. In 1938, along with the other great railway companies, it was nationalised to become part of the Société National du Chemin de Fer.

At the time of its introduction in 1909 this PO, *Decapod*, was among the most powerful locomotives in Europe. It was designed to be able to haul loads of 1,200 tonnes at 45 kph. It was also often used on passenger services. No. 6065 sits alongside the Mériller roundabout in the Dordogne.

PO poster.

Private Operators

The freight market in France was opened up to private operators in 2005 – initially for international freight and a year later for domestic freight. The first operator to obtain a licence was Europorte. This is Europorte's Vossloh Euro 4000 locomotive No. 4003 with a southbound tank train, passing through Tournus in 2015.

Colas Rail worked as a maintenance company before branching out into the carriage of freight. They have since retrenched and are now mainly concerned once more with maintenance contracts. One of their Vossloh BB 1206 machines is seen in 2009.

Voies Ferrées Locales et Industrielles (VFLI) was created in 1998 as a wholly owned low-cost subsidiary of SNCF. A Class 66 stands with a short train of timber wagons at Corbigny in 2008.

Euro Cargo Rail, which was created in 2005, was an offshoot of English Welsh and Scottish Railways (EWS). It subsequently became part of Deutsche Bahn when the parent company was acquired. A Euro Cargo Class 66 passes south through Corgoloin in April 2016.

Compagnie ferroviaire régionale was set up in 2010 as the first *opérateur ferroviaire de proximité*. From its base at Cercy-la-Tour its main business was hauling ballast from a number of quarries in the area. Vossloh G 1000 No. 1595 powers through Fours with a loaded train in April 2011.

Purrey

Valentin Purrey had previously built steam trams for the Paris tramway system. The French mainline railway companies were interested in this type of vehicle, as a means of reducing costs on lightly used services. In 1903 the PO took receipt of two three-axled Purrey *automotrices*, which, after trials where speeds of 75 kph were achieved, were allocated to the La Flèche–Sablé line. Satisfied with the results thus far obtained, the PO put in a further order to Purrey. These vehicles were of a completely different type, being in effect a truck and trailer arrangement, rather like an articulated lorry. The truck was two-axled and consisted of a driving cab, together with the boiler and engine, and the fuel and water supplies. The engine was a four-cylinder tandem compound, with chain drive to the rear axle of the truck. The trailer had only a single axle and could accommodate fifty-five passengers. There was also a luggage compartment. There were ten of these vehicles (AV2–11) plus two spare trucks. On trials between Bretigny and Dourdan one of these *automotrices* reached 85 kph running as a single unit, 70 kph hauling one trailer, and 65 kph with three. The vehicles were not used after 1914. Seven were later converted to trailers.

In 1905 the Etat received two two-axled *automotrices* from Purrey, seating twenty-four with twelve standing. They were put in service on the line from Bordeaux-Etat to André-de-Cubzac.

Around the same time as the PO, the PLM also ordered two *automotrices* (VAcf 1, 2) from Purrey. These were two-axled vehicles which could carry forty-eight passengers. Favourably impressed by their performance, the PLM ordered four more vehicles (Vacf 3-6) of a similar but slightly more powerful type. In 1907, the company then ordered ten truck/trailers, together with three additional trucks (Vacf 23–25) of a type almost identical to that of the PO. The trailers could accommodate fifty-nine passengers. Few of these vehicles saw service after the First World War.

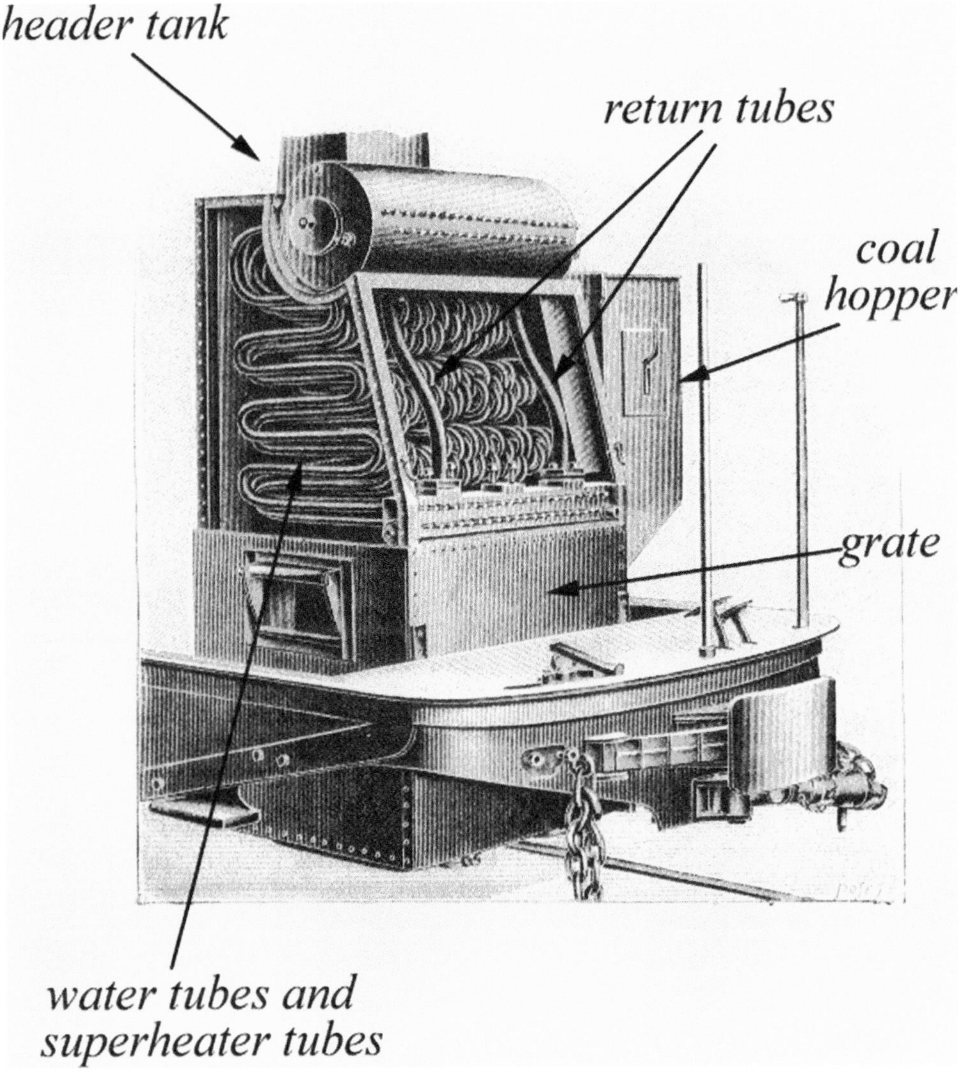

The principles of operation of the Purrey boiler.

Q

151TQ

The series 151TQ 1–22 was the last type of steam locomotive ever built for SNCF. Constructed by Corpet-Louvet, these were two-cylinder simple engines designed for freight work. They had a driving wheel diameter of 1,350 mm (4 feet 5 inches) and a top speed of 70 kph. The first ten were constructed between 1940 and 1942 and allocated to Bobigny depot, but were then requisitioned by the occupying power. A further twelve were constructed between 1946 and 1952. They were used in the Nord region and on the Grande Ceinture. The last was withdrawn in 1968 and none have been preserved.

R

Record breakers

In 1955, on 28 March, CC7107 broke the world speed record for rail with a speed of 331 kilometres per hour. The following day BB9004 achieved the same speed. The record-breaking runs took place between Facture and Morcenx on the Dax–Bordeaux main line. The two locomotives are seen here in the Cité du Train at Mulhouse.

S

Schneider

A major name in the production of railway locomotives was that of Schneider at Le Creusot, Saône et Loire. The first locomotive constructed was *La Gironde* – one of six 2-2-2s built for the Chemin de Fer Paris à Versailles in 1838. By 1855 production had risen to an average of fifty locomotives per year. A large proportion of these were exported, including, in 1865, sixteen locomotives for the Great Eastern Railway – ten 2-4-0s and six 2-2-2s. In 1876 Schneider manufactured the first compounds, these being three 0-4-2 tanks designed by Anatole Mallet for the Bayonne–Anglet–Biarritz railway. In 1891 the first 4-4-0s were built and in 1910 the first superheated engines. There was a hiatus during the First World War due to the production needs of the military, but from 1919 locomotive construction recommenced, with a total of 1,359 engines being produced in the thirteen years to 1932. These were of thirty different types and included classes 231C, D and F, and 241C for the PLM. Production slackened off during the 1930s and revived during the Second World War when output included eighty-five 2-10-0s for the Deutsche Reichsbahn. Bombing damage and sabotage delayed the resumption of production, but in 1948 the first of thirty-five 241P locomotives was constructed. One of this batch, No. 241P17, famously resides in the goods shed at Le Creusot-Ville. The last steam locomotives to be built were a batch of 2-8-4s for Brazil. Altogether Schneider had manufactured nearly 5,000 steam locomotives.

Schneider built its first electric locomotive in 1900 and its first diesel – 4CMD, destined for the PLM, in 1934. Most diesels were exported. Among the 789 electric locomotives built at Le Creusot were BB and 2D2 types for the PO and Classes BB 12000, 16000, 8100, and 25100 for SNCF. BB 12069 is currently in the custody of the group responsible for No. 241P17 and also resides at Le Creusot-Ville. One of the most famous locomotives to emerge from the works is BB 9004, joint holder of the world railway speed record from 1955 to 1981.

Part of the vast Schneider empire at Le Creusot. Almost everything seen here no longer exists.

No. 2524 was one of Schneider's products for the PLM. Built in 1910–11, it was one of a large class of four-cylinder compounds built by several companies beside Schneider. It had five-foot-10-inch driving wheels and a top speed of 110 kph.

At Autun, on 23 October 2007, No. 241p17 uses its 216 tonnes to test a newly built bridge.

Marc Seguin

Marc Seguin is credited with being the inventor of the first steam locomotive in France. He was born in Annonay on 20 April 1786. His mother was Marie-Augustine-Thérèse de Montgolfier, sister of the famous Montgolfier brothers of ballooning fame, Etienne and Joseph. In 1799, Marc was sent to Paris to be educated under the supervision of his uncle Joseph. In 1805, he returned to Annonay to work in his father's textile business. He married a Montgolfier cousin in 1813 and would go on to have thirteen children with her. Engineering was always close to Seguin's heart and in 1823 he constructed a small suspension bridge across the River Cance, using cables rather than the more conventional chains to support the bridge. In 1824, Seguin was authorised to construct a suspension bridge across the Rhône, between Tournon and Tain. This bridge, of two spans of 85 m, cost 100,000 fr to build, a considerable saving on the cost of a conventional stone bridge. The Seguin brothers would go on to build a total of 185 suspension bridges in France and elsewhere. The existing bridge at Tournon, dating from 1847, was the second built there by the Seguin brothers. The original was demolished in 1965. The oldest surviving Seguin bridge is at Andance. Built in 1827 it also spans the Rhône and is slightly longer than the first Tournon bridge at 185 m.

In 1825 Seguin and his brothers formed a company to undertake haulage by steam tug along the Rhône between Lyon and Arles. The venture was not a success and the business was dissolved in 1828. Before this the brothers had turned their attention to the railway, forming in 1826, along with Edouard Biot, a company '*du chemin de fer de Saint Etienne à Lyon*'. In both 1825 and 1827 Marc Seguin visited England, during the course of which he purchased two locomotives from the Stephensons. After studying these engines he produced his own design and in 1827 filed a patent for a design of tubular locomotive boiler. The patent was granted in February 1828 and trials of the first locomotive were made that year. The Seguin locomotive was designed with a return flue, only the return section being multi-tubular. Another radical difference to the classic Stephensonian locomotive was that instead of the air being drawn through the fire by the blast pipe, it was blown into the fire by two large fans. Seguin claimed that his locomotive was both more efficient and cheaper to construct than the Stephenson locomotives.

As for the St-Etienne railway, this was opened in stages between 1830 and 1832. The construction of this 56-kilometre railway was an enormous undertaking for the time, and included what was at that time the longest tunnel in Europe at 1.5 km. It was by no means clear that haulage on the railway would be other than by horse – the idea being that the trains would freewheel down to Lyon and be hauled back by horse. In fact, horsepower was used in part as late as 1844. Seguin constructed a total of twelve locomotives, none of which remained in service very long, all being either scrapped or rebuilt by 1843. Before that Seguin had fallen out with the railway's directors and parted company with them in 1835.

In that year Seguin effectively retired, although he was only forty-nine. He would spend the rest of his life in research and writing. In 1836 his wife Augustine died and Seguin withdrew to the Abbé de Fontenay, the property of his brother-in-law, Elie de Montgolfier. In 1838 Marc married Elie's daughter, another Augustine, thirty-two years his junior, with whom he had a further six children. Seguin was long in retirement, dying on 24 February 1875 at the age of eighty-nine.

A replica of Seguin's first locomotive, exhibited on the Champs d'Elysées in 2003.

Signals

Above left: Mechanical signalling survives in a number of places, essentially in rural locations on quiet lines, as here on the line between Auxerre and Laroche-Migennes. An AGC unit with a service for Laroche-Migennes heads north past the signals controlling the entry to Monteau-Gurgy – the station the train has just left. The red disc is a stop signal, but may be passed at slow speed with the driver being prepared to stop at the next signal, which is indicated by the yellow diamond.

Above right: Another yellow *avertissement* is seen at Châteaudun, this time accompanied by a *carré*, which is a stop signal that cannot be passed. On the adjacent line is a *violet*, which is also a stop signal but is only seen on sidings. An X 72500 unit heads away southwards on 31 June 2014. The mechanical signals at Châteaudun have now been replaced by colour lights.

At St-Denis-près-Martel, on 15 April 2013, single unit No. X73726 approaches the station past a fine display of *carrés* and *avertissements*. On the left there is also a *violet*.

The lever frame on the platform at St-Denis-près-Martel.

SNCF

The Société National des Chemins de Fer Français (SNCF) was formed in 1938. It took under its control the former private companies: the PO-Midi, PLM, Etat, Est, AL and Nord. The total route kilometres at that time was 42,612 and there were 515,000 employees. Taken into SNCF ownership were 17,765 steam locomotives, 728 electric locomotives, 405 *automotrices electriques* (EMUs), 658 *autorails* (DMUs), four diesel locomotives, 30,496 carriages, 8,074 *fourgons* and 474,313 freight wagons. Initial organisation was by region, based on the former companies' areas. These were Est (incorporating Est and AL), Sud-Est (PLM), Sud-Ouest (PO), Nord (Nord), and Ouest (Etat).

Over the years the national company has undergone much change and reorganisation. Currently there are two main organisations: SNCF Réseau and SNCF Mobilités. SNCF Réseau is responsible for the track and other infrastructure. Its locomotives are painted yellow and branded 'Infra'. SNCF Mobilités is further divided into SNCF Voyages, Keolis and SNCF Logistics. The constituent parts of SNCF Mobilités are TGV, TER, Transilien,

Wearing an earlier form of the SNCF logo is No. 67593, heading south through St-Pierre-le-Moutier in October 2014.

and Intercités. Keolis is responsible for urban transport. SNCF Logistics is the freight arm and includes SNCF Fret, VFLI and a number of smaller companies.

A significant date came in 1981 with the opening of the first Ligne de Grande Vitesse between Paris and Lyon. The TGV has been a great success story for SNCF and there are now 2,800 km of high-speed lines, approximately 10 per cent of the total route mileage of 28,000. Currently SNCF has 146,000 employees, runs 15,000 trains every day carrying 5 million passengers, and manages 3,000 stations.

On the same day, further south at Chantenay-St-Imbert, No. 167441 passes through, wearing the latest version of the logo. For an example of a locomotive bearing the original *macaron* logo of SNCF see page 17.

Streamliner

In 1934 the PLM decided to introduce a streamlined train on the Paris–Lyon–Marseille axis. The locomotives chosen to haul the trains were the Atlantics of the series 2971–2990 (221A). Two machines, Nos 221A 11 and 14, were extensively rebuilt. This rebuild included the fitting of a superheater, modified piston valves, an ACFI-feed water heater and a mechanical lubricator, plus other modifications and, of course, a streamlined casing. The engines were also supplied with a new bogie tender of greater capacity. Trials were successful and showed that the streamlining gave a considerable reduction in resistance. On one trial a speed of 156 kph was reached. The trials were carried out with just three carriages, also streamlined, but there was sufficient power in reserve to add a fourth for the service trains.

A further five locomotives were rebuilt, the class becoming 221 B. The later engines had a modified form of streamlining, which left the motion uncovered. A number of trains ran on the Paris–Lyon and Paris–Evian routes from 1935, but the full service to Marseille did not start until May 1937. Train No. 11 left Paris at 12.00 and arrived in Marseille at 21.05. Train No. 12 left Marseille at 09.55 and arrived in Paris at 19.00. There were five stops, which took a total of 18 minutes. Engines were changed at Lyon-Perrache.

The train became a victim of its own success. The rake consisted of one first, two second and a *restaurant-fourgon* car, giving a total of just 192 places. The locomotives were insufficiently powerful for further carriages to be added, and in 1938 the streamlined train was replaced by a conventional service hauled by a Pacific.

No. 221B 14 at Laroche-Migennes during trails.

No. 221B 15 at Besançon. Notice the modified form of streamlining, as applied to the later engines.

T

TAR

In 1933 the Nord company ordered from the Société Franco-Belge two three-coach diesel-electric multiple units. The two end vehicles (*motrices*) carried at their outer ends a Maybach V12 GO5 diesel engine of 380 hp – the same engine, incidentally, with which the Flying Hamburger trains were equipped. The engine drove a Siemens generator supplying current to two traction motors situated on the inner bogie of the *motrices*. The middle vehicle was an unpowered trailer. The two *motrices* provided both first- and second-class accommodation, while the trailer was exclusively second class. Streamlining was a feature of the design, not just in the rounded shape of the outer ends but also in the attention to irregular surfaces along the length of the train. The carriages were painted in a two-tone grey livery. In addition to the conventional brakes the trains were equipped with *patins* – brake shoes to act on the rails in an emergency. Top speed was 140 kph.

The trains started regular service with the 1934/5 winter timetable. The Nord must have been well pleased with their trains because in 1935 the company ordered a further nineteen *motrices* and eight trailers. There were a number of differences to the original pair. The *motrices* were slightly longer and carried an up-rated Maybach engine of 410 hp (GO56). The creation of SNCF in 1938 put paid to any further orders and the outbreak of the Second World War led to the cessation of all services by TAR. Services resumed after the war, including between Paris and Lyon-Perrache. This non-stop service – trains Nos 41 and 42 – completing the 512-kilometre distance in 5 hours and 7 minutes was a world record for non-stop running for trains of this type, and a world record for all trains for average speed. The succeeding years saw the TAR duties gradually replaced by other forms of motive power and the very last train ran between Lille and Paris on 30 May 1959. The *motrices* were all scrapped, while a few of the trailers remained in use as service vehicles.

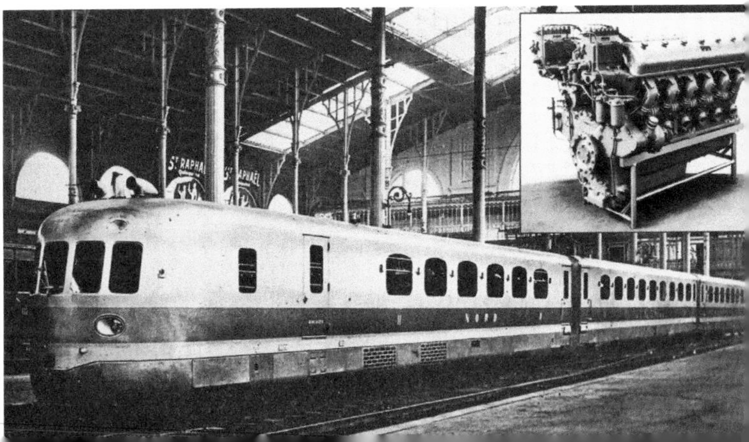

A TAR stands at Gare du Nord. The inset shows the Maybach engine.

TER

The branding Transport Express Régional was first conceived in 1984, since which time the regional councils have been taking ever greater control and responsibility for financing services within their regions, which includes specifying service and fare levels. Currently there are approximately 5,000 TER trains daily, carrying 800,000 passengers. Fares are heavily subsidised, with only 28 per cent of costs being covered by fare receipts.

On 1 April 2014 a TER Bourgogne AGC unit departs from Luzy with a Nevers–Dijon working. There are twelve or thirteen services daily on this line, though not all stop at Luzy.

Trains de Grande Vitesse

Research on high-speed lines began in the 1960s, but construction work on the TGV did not begin until 1976. The first line to be completed was from Paris to Lyon and the first public services started in September 1981. There are a number of different TGV trainsets. The first was the TGV Sud-Est (eight-car dual-voltage), which has been followed by Lyria (eight-car triple-voltage), TGV Duplex (eight-car dual-voltage double-deck), TGV Atlantique (ten-car dual-voltage), TGV Réseau (eight-car dual-voltage), TGV Réseau-Duplex (eight-car dual-voltage double-deck), TGV Dasye (eight-car dual-voltage double-deck), TGV Euroduplex (ten-car triple-voltage double-deck). TGV Sud-Est and TGV Atlantique sets have a top speed of 300 kph; the others are 320 kph. A TGV set holds the world-speed record for rail at 574.8 kph, which was achieved on 3 April 2007.

The existing Lignes de Grande Vitesse are: Sud-Est, Rhin-Rhône, Est, Atlantique, Nord, Sud-Europe Atlantique, and Bretagne-Pays de la Loire, giving a total of 2,651 km (2017). Further lines are planned.

Above left: In original orange livery, this TGV is seen at Andelot in May 1998 on the first day of the Paris Gare de Lyon–Lausanne service. (Graham Skinner)

Above right: Old and new. Between Auneau and Bonneval the classic line from Paris to Tours via Vendôme runs alongside the LGV Atlantique. In 2014 a pair of TGV Atlantique sets head towards Paris.

Seen in April 2015, this is Duplex set No. 748 at the 'triangle de Coubert'. The train is a Bordeaux–Lille service and has a single-deck TGV at the rear. The train is a cross-country service that left the LGV Atlantique at Massy-Palaiseau and travelled eastbound past Orly to Valenton where it joined the LGV Sud-Est. After Brie-Comte-Robert the train took the east branch of the triangle and is seen here heading north to Marne-la-Vallée. Later it will join the LGV Nord for Lille. (Graham Skinner)

Thuile

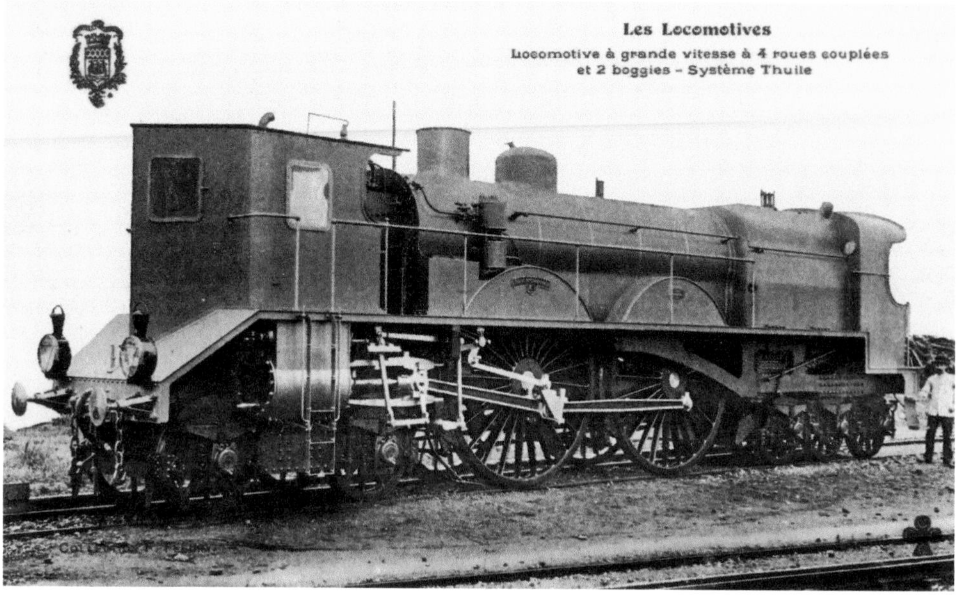

Les Locomotives
Locomotive à grande vitesse à 4 roues couplées
et 2 boggies - Système Thuile

A number of unusual locomotives found their way out of the Schneider works. In 1900 the Thuile locomotive appeared. This was a 4-4-6, which had 2.5-metre (8-foot-2-inch) driving wheels and a driving cab forward of the smokebox. It was accompanied by a ten-wheel tender and weighed 138 tonnes. The engine had a tendency to derail and on one of these occasions, during trial running between Chartres and Orleans, the designer, M. Thuile, was thrown from the engine and killed. The engine was returned to the Schneider works where it was broken up in 1904.

Tours

The Paris–Orleans Company (PO) had opened its line to Orleans in 1843. The Orleans–Bordeaux Company (OB) came into being in 1844, and by 1846 had completed the line to Tours. The station in Tours – known as the *embarcadère* – was a terminus shared by three companies: the PO, the OB and the Tours–Nantes(TN) company. It had two platform lines and four centre roads. In fact, the PO had a separate entrance to the other two, but this inconvenience was addressed in 1852 by the merger of the three companies. From 1875 the Compagnie de la Vendée (later part of the Réseau de l' Etat) had a separate station in Tours, adjacent to that of the PO. This was known as the *débarcadère*. The PO's *embarcadère* and the Etat's *débarcadère* continued to function as separate entities, but the situation was slightly ridiculous in that the PO line from Loches terminated in the Etat station, while the Etat line from Sagré terminated in that of the PO.

Towards the end of the century it was agreed that a single unified station should be built. The architect was Victor Laloux. Thus, in 1898, came into being the magnificent station that we see today, which still retains its original train shed, 62 metres long, accommodating the eight platform lines and also, thankfully, its beautiful frontage. The interior walls are decorated with eighteen tiled murals depicting some of the destinations served by the station. Since 1984 the station has been classified as a *monument historique*.

Above left: The original *débarcadère*.

Above right: Victor Laloux's station of 1898.

One of the tiled murals.

U

Unfinished

Two railways with very similar stories. The greatest similarity being that they were railways that were constructed but on which no train ever ran.

The Transcevenole

In the mid-nineteenth century two options were considered for the prolongation of the railway beyond Clermont-Ferrand – either via Langogne and Alès to Nîmes, or via le Puy, Aubenas and Le Teil. As history shows, the first was chosen, but there were still those, particularly the local politicians, who campaigned for the second to be built. Finally, in 1906, a line from Le Puy to Nieigles-Prades (the former name of Lalevade-de-l'Ardèche) was declared of *utilité publique*, but work did not start for another five years and was then interrupted by the First World War. Work restarted in 1919, mainly at the instigation of André Laurent-Eynac, a local politician and minister in the Poincaré government. Work was concentrated on the section of line in Haute-Loire – that is to say as far as Présailles, apart from the tunnels of St-Cirques (later named Roux) and Cheylas, both in the Ardèche. By 1932 nearly 130 million francs had been spent on the project, and at this point the Conseil National Economique decided that, until further notice, only the 22.2-kilometre section from Le Puy to Le Monastier-sur-Gazeille should be completed. In 1936 the line was structurally complete, the stations and crossing keepers' cottages built, a layer of ballast put down, and rails and sleepers stocked ready to be laid. However, at this moment the minister of public works decided that no further work should take place. The section beyond Monastier was officially abandoned in 1937, and the section thereto in 1941.

The Transcévenole was an extraordinarily heavily engineered line. In its 93-kilometre length there would have been fifteen stations, twelve viaducts, thirty-five tunnels, 319 smaller bridges and sixty level crossings. The longest tunnels were those of St-Cirques (Roux, 3,336 m) and Présailles (2,626 m), the latter remaining uncompleted. The majority of the tunnels, no less than twenty-six, were to have been in the section of line in the Ardèche. Also in the *département* was to have been the most extraordinary feature of the line, the triple spiral near Montpezat-sur-Bauzon, an engineering feat that would have been unique in Europe. This 19-kilometre switchback, in a distance as the crow flies of just 5 kilometres, would have been undertaken to lift the railway some 700 m.

The viaduct of Recoumène, 250 metres long, 65.6 metres high, built between 1921 and 1925. The absence of any railings makes for a nervous crossing for those of a vertiginous disposition.

The station of Lantriac, which never saw a train.

Albi to St-Affrique

As early as 1875 a line had been projected to connect Albi with Vigan, in the Gard, where it would make an end-on connection with the PLM network – the aim being to connect the Tarn coalfield with eastern Languedoc and Provence. The section from Tournemire-Roquefort to Vigan was completed in 1896, but in the meantime enthusiasm had waned for the section from Albi to St-Affrique. (The section from Tournemire to St-Affrique had been completed some years earlier.) However, at St-Juery a foundry offered the finance to build the line from Albi as far as its works just beyond St-Juery. The offer was accepted, with work starting in 1896, leading to the opening in 1899. The initial passenger service was of four return trains per day, later reduced to two. The main users were the workers at the foundry. This passenger service ceased in 1933 and the line became essentially an industrial branch, serving a number of clients, as well as the foundry. All traffic ceased in 2004 but in January 2012 RFF announced a 'probable' renovation of the line and it is reported that there are a number of potential clients keen to make use of rail (see map, page 11).

As for the section St-Juery–St-Affrique, work started only in 1904. It was then delayed by the First World War and not completed until 1932, at which time the Midi had lost all interest in the line. The company was given permission by the Conseil National Economique to postpone the installation of track and signalling, which would have completed the work. The work was never done, and thus this line – 66.7 km in length, with nineteen tunnels, seven viaducts, fourteen stations, crossing cottages, and numerous other *ouvrages d'art* – was never to see a train run, and was declassified in 1941. The total cost of the works thus far carried out amounted to 63.7 million francs.

The beautiful Viaduc de Courris.

The tunnel of Lincou. As here, much of the railway trackbed is now a road.

V

Viaducts and Bridges

Chaumont Viaduct is on the main line between Paris Est and Mulhouse. It was built in just fifteen months between 1855 and 1856. It consists of fifty arches and is 600 metres long and 52 metres high. It was partly destroyed by German forces in 1944 and rebuilt in 1945.

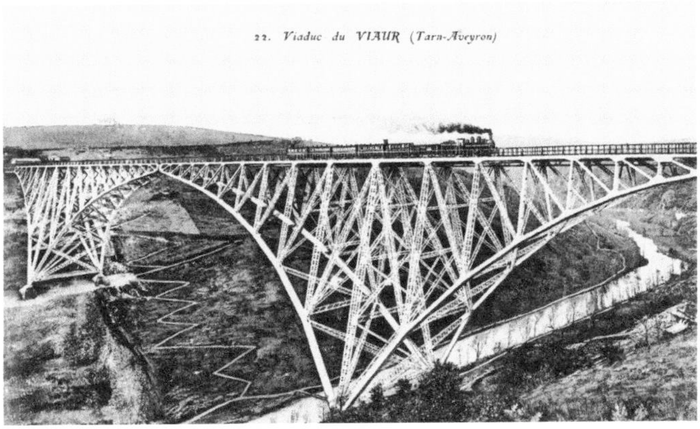

The viaduct crossing the valley of the Viaur on the Carmaux–Rodez line is the largest steel bridge in France. It took five years to build and was completed in 1902. It is 460 metres long, 116 metres high and weighs 3,800 tonnes.

Above left: Mussy Viaduct is on the line between Lyon and Paray-le-Monial and was built between 1892 and 1895. It consists of eighteen arches and is 561 metres long and 60 metres high.

Above right: The Port Aubry bridge across the Loire was constructed in 1893 as part of the line linking Bourges and Cosne-sur-Loire. It was intended primarily for military purposes and is 828 metres long and consists of fourteen spans of 58 metres. It was bombed in 1944 and subsequently rebuilt. The last train ran in 2000 and it is today used by the Cyclorail du Sancerrois.

The Viaduc des Fades is on the line from Lapeyrouse to Volvic where it crosses the valley of the Sioule. It was constructed between 1901 and 1909 and at that time it was the highest viaduct in the world. It remains the highest viaduct in France, and the two masonry piers that support it, at 92 metres, are the tallest masonry piers anywhere. It is 470.25 metres long and weighs 2,604 tonnes. It was designed by Félix Virard and is a *monument historique*. Due to lack of maintenance it has been in poor condition for many years, necessitating its crossing only by light vehicles at much reduced speed. Finally, in 2007 it was taken out of use altogether.

The Pont de Pruniers carried the Petit Anjou metre-gauge line across the Maine. It was one of the few bridges across the river not destroyed by the retreating German forces in 1944. Thus, it allowed the American army of General Patton to cross the Maine, liberate Angers, and more importantly head off German forces coming up from the south-west. There is a plaque on the bridge that reads: '*5ème division d'infanterie de l'armee des Etats-Unis a franchi la Maine sur ce pont le 8 aout 1944 pour liberer Angers. commemoration avec les veterans americains, le 9 mai 1987.*'

The Viaduc du Gabarit was constructed by Gustav Eiffel between 1882 and 1884. It crosses the Truyère on the electrified railway line, the 'Aubrac', which runs from Beziers to Neussargues. It is 565 metres long, stands 124 metres above the river and weighs 3,587 tonnes. Trains crossing it are restricted to a maximum speed of 10 kph.

W

War

The railways figured little in the Franco-Prussian War of 1870, except in being found wanting when troops needed to be urgently rushed to the front. Determined not to be in the same position a second time, the French government ordered the railways to make sufficient provision for the rapid movement and deployment of troops and materiel. Many new lines were built, the sole purpose of which was to provide alternative routes in the case of a principal route being blocked or congested. These *rocades*, having very little commercial traffic, were often the first to be closed. Certain stations were designated *gares regulatrices.* These were the focal points for the movement of troops and supplies to the front.

At the outbreak of the First World War, Is-sur-Tille was designated as one of these *gare regulatrices.* Mobilisation saw the passage in a few weeks of 314,084 troops and 9,361 officers. In the seventeen days between 7 and 24 September, 443 trains passed through the station. After this hectic period Is settled down as a transit station for munitions and other supplies. By 1915 there were 4,000 m^2 of warehouses of various kinds, plus a postal depot. The existing sidings were greatly enlarged. The American entry into the war in 1917 brought a vast increase in the facilities at Is. By the time of the Armistice, 175 km of railway lines had been laid, 390 warehouses built, and 250 barracks constructed. Between 1917 and 1920, 2 million American soldiers and 4 million tonnes of freight had passed through Is-sur-Tille.

As well as the *gare regulatrices* there were many *gares militaires.* Very often these consisted of a simple platform, away from the normal stations, where loading or unloading could take place. Before the outbreak of the First World War considerable planning had gone into the movement to the front of 800,000 men, 200,000 horses, plus their equipment and supplies, all of which had to be achieved in eleven days, and in fact was done so. The war brought the expected destruction, part of it caused by the retreating French army, which blew up bridges to slow the advance of the German troops. Suffice to say that the railways played a considerable and essential role in the movement of troops and supplies throughout the war.

Part of the Armistice agreement was for the German railways to supply their French counterparts with 5,000 locomotives and 150,000 wagons as part of war reparations. It was stipulated that these were to be the most modern locomotives in the best condition and the transfer had to be achieved in just thirty-one days. As part of the post-war treaty, Alsace-Lorraine was to be returned to France, which included all of the rolling stock and motive power of the railways of that region. In 1940 the tables were turned when the

German occupiers demanded that 1,000 locomotives should be sent to Germany. This was in addition to the entire stock of the Alsace-Lorraine network, which was once again part of Germany. This was just the start of things, and by the end of the war no less than 3,315 locomotives had made their way from France to Germany, comprising one-third of all SNCF locomotives. As well as this, in excess of 5,000 carriages and a quarter of a million wagons were 'borrowed' by the German authorities.

In addition to the pillaging were several waves of destruction. First was that caused by retreating Allied troops in an attempt to slow the German advance. The next wave was caused by the extensive bombing by the Allies, intended to stop the enemy from rapidly bringing up troops to confront the Allies on the Normandy beachheads and to impede the movement of German troops generally. There had been some bombing attacks before this, but the greatest concentration was in the months from April to June 1944. The bombing was effective in that the railways were completely dislocated but it also resulted in the deaths of more than 68,000 civilians and the destruction of hundreds of thousands of homes. There were, in addition, acts of sabotage by railwaymen and the resistance. The third wave was carried out by the retreating German army, which not only destroyed bridges and viaducts but blew up whole stations, depots and any facility that might be useful to the advancing Allies. During the conflict more than 8,938 SNCF employees lost their lives and a great many were imprisoned in Germany.

Above left: The Pont des Dombes was blown up by the retreating German forces in August 1944. It was rebuilt the following year.

Above right: Another piece of destruction accomplished in the same year was the blowing up of Dijon station.

Above left: The First World War saw the same tactics. Jeumont is just over the border from Belgium. The French army has blown up the railway bridge in order to impede the advance of the German forces in 1914. German engineers have built the replacement, which can be seen behind.

Above right: Work is in hand on the enlargement of the *gare regulatrice* of Is-sur-Tille.

Above left: An intriguing image from the same conflict. This is the American supply depot at Nevers. On the right is a German prisoner of war, crossing the 50-cm tracks – part of the layout used within the depot. In the centre are two American soldiers and, behind them, most interesting of all, is what is clearly a McIntosh Caledonian Railway-designed locomotive. Whether it is Belgian or British, or its class, is impossible to say. (Gallica)

Above right: In 1944 the Allies bombed the town of Le Creusot several times. Their target was the Schneider works. Considerable damage was done to the surrounding area. In order to clear some of the debris, 50-cm tracks were laid in the town and, as seen here, German Feldbahn 0-8-0 locomotives were used to haul the trains.

French railway workers were in the forefront of the Allied bombing. These reinforced-concrete individual air-raid shelters were provided at many locations.

One of the Armistice locomotives acquired by the Etat network, originally XII H2 3707 of the Saxony network. This became SNCF No. 230E 977.

Now in the hands of a German driver is No. 230A 475, originally an Est locomotive of the series 3401–3500, dating from the period 1898–1902. This was one of the many locomotives requisitioned by the occupying forces during the Second World War.

X

X = *Autorail*

Autorail is the collective name for both diesel multiple units and single diesel units. All *autorails* have a number preceded by the letter X. A selection of *autorails* both old and modern are shown here.

Unifié 150ch (X5500/5800)

The idea for a lightweight, standard *autorail* for duty on less-used lines goes back to the formation of the Division des Etudes des Autorails, shortly after the creation of SNCF. Its director, Charles Tourneur, was charged with both the rationalisation of the existing fleet of 850 *autorails* and with the planning of the new types, which would ultimately replace much of this fleet, as well as steam locomotives. He suggested that there should be three standard (*unifié*) types of 150, 300 and 600 hp. The first 150 hp prototype appeared in March 1947 (X 7029, later X 5010) and the second in August (X 7030, later X 5011). Series production began in 1950 and continued until 1955. A total of 107 units were produced, including the two prototypes. All construction was by Régie Nationale des Usines Renault (RNUR) but two different engines were fitted – either the 150 hp six-cylinder Renault 561B of 15.6 litres, or the 160 hp six-cylinder Saurer BXDS of 15.2 litres. The engines were mounted transversely and transmission to the four-speed mechanical gearbox was by conventional friction clutch. The fact that only the third and fourth gears had synchromesh implies some nifty double-declutching by the driver. Somewhat unusually, these *autorails* had four independent axles arranged in pairs instead of the more conventional bogies. The engine drove the inside axle of the nearest pair. The maximum speed was 90 kph.

Withdrawals started in 1969, and by 1977 just six members of the class were active. These six were loaned to CFD at Autun and were used between Autun and Etang, Autun

One of the preserved units, the property of Agrivap, is seen at Sembadel in 2016.

and Epinac, and Autun, Montchanin and Montçeau-les-Mines. All were withdrawn by 1978. Two X 5500 and eight X 5800 survive in preservation.

Unifié 300ch (X3800), 'Picasso'

The Unifié 300ch, more commonly known as the 'Picasso' was built between 1950 and 1961 by three different manufacturers: RNUR, De Dietrich and Ateliers de Construction du Nord de la France. They were equipped with one of three different power units: Renault 517G (300 hp), Renault 575 (340 hp) or Saurer BZDS (320 hp). The Renault 517 dated back to 1936 and was installed in innumerable *autorails* both in France and abroad. Transmission was via a mechanical gearbox, which involved double-declutching, and thus considerable skill on the part of the driver. The top speed of all units was 120 kph. The interior was configured for either sixty-two second class, or thirty-two second class and twenty first class. There was space for 2.5 tonnes of luggage. A total of 251 were built, all being withdrawn by 1988, although at least twenty-five remain in preservation.

Two of the preserved units are seen on a special train in 2012 shortly after leaving Etang and heading for Autun.

Unifié 600ch (X2400)

The superpower X2400 single units appeared between 1951 and 1955. They were constructed by Decauville, equipped with two Renault 517G 32-litre V12 engines and gave a total of 600 hp. Seventy-nine units were built, the last being withdrawn in 1989. At 27.73 metres (91 feet), they were the longest single units produced for SNCF. They could carry eighty passengers and 2.5 tonnes of luggage at a top speed of 120 kph. Despite their size and the presence of the two massive Renault engines, they weighed only 42.5 tonnes. They were originally built to accommodate three classes of passenger. They were capable of hauling up to three trailers, depending on the severity of the gradients encountered.

Twelve units have been preserved. One of these, X 2403, is seen at Laizy-Brion station with a special working in June 2009.

EAD, *Caravelle*

The EAD was introduced in 1963 as a two-car unit, consisting of a powered unit and a trailer. There were two prototypes: X4300 and X4500. The only difference between the two was the engine fitted. The former had a six-cylinder turbo-charged SSCM Poyaud C6150SrHT engine of some 19 litres, giving 435 hp. The latter had a Saurer SDHR engine, also six-cylinders and turbo-charged, giving 448 hp. The engines were underfloor mounted. Both types drove an eight-speed De Dietrich gearbox through a hydraulic clutch. Their top speed was 120 kph. Both power cars could seat sixty passengers in second class. Trailers were of two types: either with twelve first-class and sixty-nine second-class seats, or twenty-four first-class and forty-nine second-class seats. A total of 151 units of Class X4300 were constructed, and 126 of Class X4500. In the 1980s a number of units of both classes were modernised. The units received a new front end and the interior was modified. Neither type remains in passenger-carrying service, although a large number were sold to Regio Trains in Rumania, where they remain in use.

Between 1971 and 1977 a further 115 units were built. These received the Saurer engine, but transmission was now by a Voith automatic gearbox. These units were numbered X4630 to 4744. The year 1975 saw a new development with the construction of the three-car units of Class X4901. There was a total of thirteen of these units, comprising two motor units equipped with the Saurer engines, sandwiching one trailer. The maximum speed was 140 kph. Six of the units were allocated to Marseille Blancarde, and seven to Sotteville. The year 1988 saw all the units at the latter location, where all remained in use in 2015. In 1977 and 1978 thirty-six *autorails* of Class X4750, and in 1981 seven of Class X4790, were produced. These were the first of the EAD family to be equipped with an uprated engine, the Saurer now giving nearly 600 hp, enabling a top speed of 140 kph.

In May 2007 a pair of units is seen near Mesvres with a Nevers–Dijon service.

X 2800

The X 2800 series of *autorails* were much loved by enthusiasts, mainly because of the throaty roar of their powerful engines. They were indeed powerful machines, being the most powerful single unit at the time they were introduced. This power was supplied by the MGO V12 54-litre engine, delivering 825 hp and giving a maximum speed of 120 kph (some units 140 kph). These *autorails* were capable of hauling up to four trailers. A total of 119 units were built between 1957 and 1962. The first sixteen came from Deacauville and the remainder from Renault. The last unit was withdrawn from service in 2009, but a large number have survived into preservation. In May 1998, X 2816 and 2853 are seen at Andelot arriving from the branch line to Morez and St-Claude. They will reverse here and depart to Dole. (Graham Skinner)

XTER and ATER

In the late 1990s SNCF introduced two new *autorails* to French railways for local services. These were Class X 72500 'XTER' (Automoteur TER) and Class X 73500 and X 73900 'ATER' (Autorail TER). Neither have been particularly successful. X 72500 are multiple units consisting of two or three cars. Built by Alstom, they were introduced in 1997. The power cars are equipped with two MAN D2866 LUE 602 six-cylinder in-line engines, giving a total of 300 kW per power car. As well as being unreliable they are also extremely noisy and do not provide a comfortable ride.

XTER unit No. X 72550 is seen at Voves in June 2014.

Classes X 73500 and X 73900 are single units – the latter equipped to work across the border into Germany. They are also powered by two MAN engines per unit but are rated at only 258 kW per car. Production was from 1999 to 2004. The units, which have a top speed of 140 kph, have acquired a number of colourful names, including 'concombre' and 'suppositoire'. Single unit No. X 73756 waits for its next turn of duty at Dole in September 2014.

Far more successful have been the AGC units from Bombardier, which were first introduced in 2005. These come in several different configurations – either diesel, diesel and electric at 1,500 V DC, or diesel and electric at both 1,500V DC and 25 kV. This unit, No. B 81500, is one of the diesel and electric 1,500 V DC units. It has arrived at St-Claude on 12 July 2014 with a service from Besançon.

Y

Y = *Locotracteur* (Shunter)

SNCF shunter numbers are preceded by the letter Y. A selection of shunters are shown here.

Above left: The Class Y 7400 was based on a successful rebuild of a Class Y 7100 machine. This large class is equipped with a Poyaud 6PYT engine and has mechanical transmission. Still in original livery, No. Y 7532 is seen at Montchanin on 28 July 2008.

Above right: Starting in 2011, Socofer, on behalf of SNCF Infra, began the modernisation of Classes Y 7100 and Y 7400. The Poyaud engine was replaced with the MAN 6LD 2066 LE621 engine, rated at 225 kW. Almost everything else was also new. Just the chassis and wheels were retained. The first twenty-two machines were rebuilt by Socofer and the rest by SNCF, using kits supplied by Socofer. A total of 110 machines have been rebuilt. No. Y 9061 is seen near Voves in June 2014 with a weed-killing train.

The Y 8000 Class was introduced in 1977 and continued to be built over the next twelve years. The first ninety were built by Moyse and the remainder by Fauvet-Girel. The machines were originally equipped with a Poyaud V12-520NS engine of 224 kW, but were later re-engined with a Renault RVI Euro 2 or Euro 3. At the same time the locomotives were turned out in Fret livery as seen in the photograph, which shows No. Y 8180 heading away from Etang-sur-Arroux in 2008.

This PLM Berliet shunter has sat rusting at Cercy-la-Tour for many years waiting for some kind person to rescue it and put it in a museum. This photograph was taken in 2009.

A large number of shunters are in industrial use. At le Teil, in the Ardèche, a Moyse shunter is at work with the weekly fertiliser train from Germany.

Z

Z = Electric Multiple Units (EMUs)

There are different French names in use for EMU, including *rame automotrice*, *élément automoteur électrique*, or simply *automotrice*. SNCF electric multiple units have a number preceded by Z. A number of units currently in use are shown here.

Above left: The Z2 units were first introduced in 1980. The Z 9500 series date from 1982 and are dual-voltage units. They are all two-car units and operate mainly east of Dijon, in the Jura and in the Alps. Unit No. Z 9652 is seen at Is-sur-Tille in 2014.

Above right: Régio 2N units made their first appearance in 2014. This dual-current, double-deck unit is intended primarily for service with the regional TER operations. The trains are articulated and come in a number of different formations, ranging from six to ten vehicles. Maximum speed also varies according to the type of use intended, from 160 to 200 kph. A six-car unit is seen heading south at Blaisy-Bas in September 2015.

Also seen at Blaisy-Bas is unit No. 27546. This is the electric version of the AGC body shell. Built by Bombardier and introduced in 2005, all are equipped to work on either 25 kV or 1,500 DC. These units consist of either three or four cars. This is a three-car unit.

Alstom's offering for regional services is the Régiolis unit. These are also dual-current, articulated trains, but in this case single deck. One of the first orders was for the Aquitaine region and here we see unit No. 51515 arriving at Facture-Biganos. Note the very characteristic Midi catenary. It was south of here that electric locomotives Nos CC 7107 and BB 9004 broke the world-speed record in 1955.